SQUARE DANCING

Clayne R. Jensen
and
Mary Bee Jensen

Brigham Young University Press

Library of Congress Cataloging in Publication Data

Jensen, Clayne R
Square dancing.

Published in 1966 under title: Beginning square dance.
Bibliography: p. 159
1. Square dancing. I. Jensen, Mary Bee, joint author.
II. Title.
GV1763.J4 1973 793.3'4 73-2436
ISBN 0-8425-0459-1

Library of Congress Catalog Card Number: 73-2436
International Standard Book Number: 0-8425-0459-1

Brigham Young University Press, Provo, Utah 84602
New, enlarged edition. First edition © by
Wadsworth Publishing Company, Inc.
Printed in the United States of America
73 5M 14029

Contents

1. Discover Values

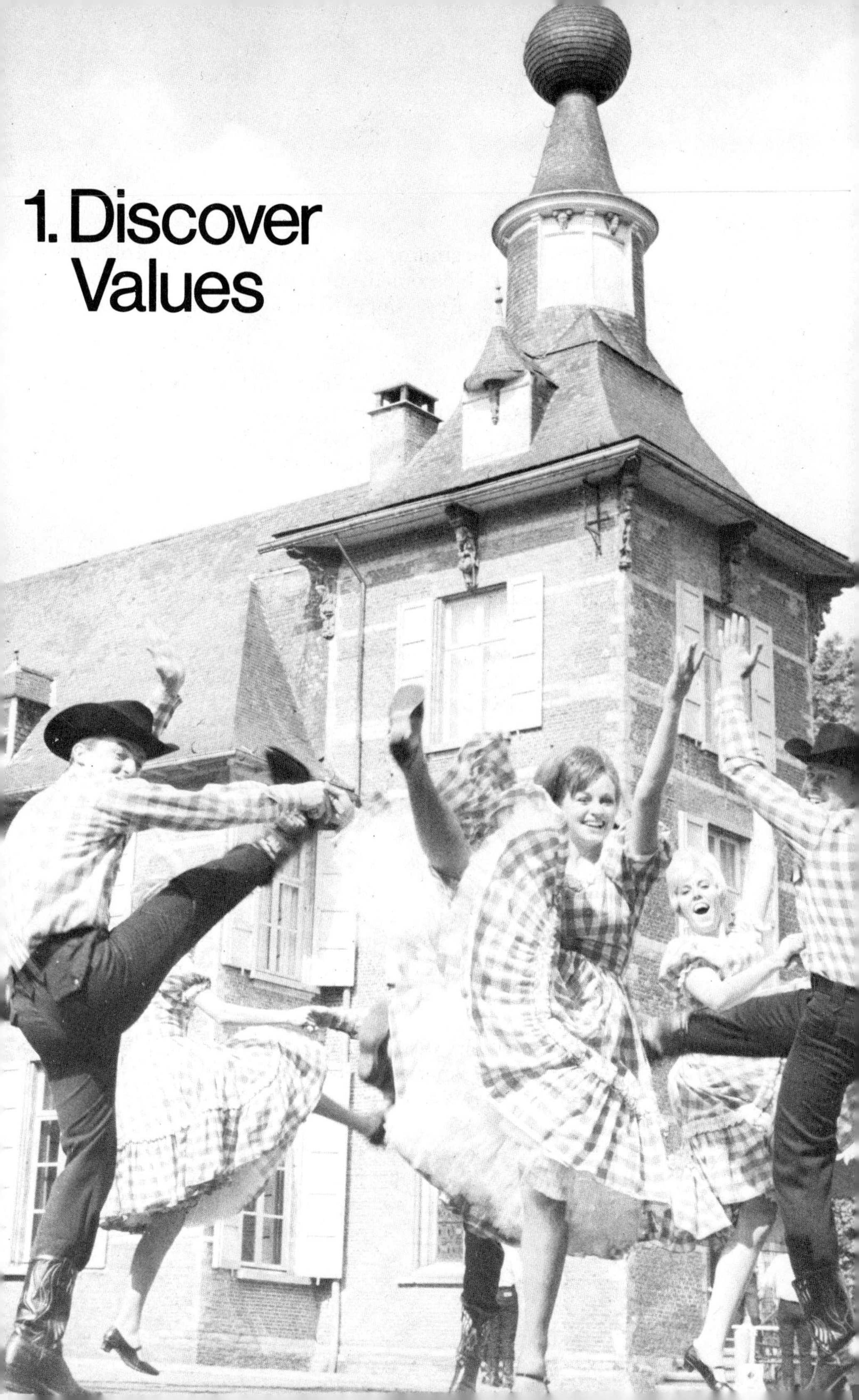

Soon after its beginning as an early American folk dance, square dancing blossomed into one of the most popular forms of dance. Ever since then, it has remained popular among Americans.

What has brought the square dance such acceptance in America? Why has it become a part of educational curricula as well as a popular club and party activity? Answers to these questions can be found by considering some values of square dancing.

SOCIAL VALUES

Square dancing is truly social in nature because the dancers change partners often during the dance, and each dancer is a member of a group consisting of seven other persons. During a square dance session, everyone dances with several different partners in several different sets.

Because square dancing is performed in couples, it gives boys and girls, or men and women, a chance to mix in a recreational activity that fosters wholesome relationships and desirable patterns of conduct.

Because of its social nature, square dancing helps to break down shyness among people and gives them an opportunity to develop new friends with mutual interests. It also encourages people to practice courtesy and develop the ability to meet and converse with others.

Because of their distinct American heritage, the dances usually have an American folk atmosphere that adds personality to a social occasion.

As a wholesome activity for leisure-time participation, the square dance is especially important now, when leisure time is more abundant than ever before in the United States.

CULTURAL VALUES

The culture of a society is made up of those values and practices which are passed on from generation to generation. Square dancing is truly part of the American culture because it originated in this country, and America has continued to be its home.

Square dancing tells much about the early settlers of America—their personalities, living patterns, and social needs. To know about square dancing is to know something about our forefathers, and about a segment of the social life that has evolved from the early settlements in this country.

This form of dance has changed in certain respects to fit the mode of the times and the changing personalities and needs of the people. But the basic fundamentals of the dance have persisted, and its basic nature has remained the same.

PHYSIOLOGICAL VALUES

Square dancing is moderately strenuous and, if done regularly, will contribute to physical fitness. Its advantage over many activities lies in its long usefulness to the individual—throughout the major portion of one's life.

Square dancing helps develop rhythm, specific neuromuscular coordinations, balance, grace, and poise.

Because of its social nature, square dancing encourages good grooming and appropriate dress.

PSYCHOLOGICAL VALUES

Many leaders in the field of mental health and social adjustment have pointed out the importance of hobbies. For many people, square dancing is the hobby they enjoy most.

Because people like to learn new skills and develop new techniques, square dancing offers the joy of achievement in an activity that contributes to the satisfaction and well-being of the individual.

For some, the satisfaction of feeling accepted in the social group of their choice is one of the chief rewards of square dancing. Such acceptance contributes to psychological stability and adjustment.

Through square dancing you may become truly recreated—refreshed emotionally, physically, and mentally. Like many other recreational activities, it can help bring your life into balance, generating enthusiasm in an otherwise routine day.

The values derived from square dancing will depend upon your interest and ability. The greatest benefit will come when you develop appreciation for the dance and learn to perform skillfully. You naturally tend to participate in activities that you perform well, and to avoid those you perform poorly. Therefore, the development of skill adds to your enthusiasm for square dancing, and the activity, in turn, serves you better.

This book is designed to help you develop skill rapidly so that square dancing may quickly become meaningful and enjoyable to you.

2. Know Square-Dancing History

Know Square-Dancing History

Dancing is as old as the history of mankind. Records of the ancient cavemen indicate they danced around the fire or across the remains of a conquered beast or enemy. In ancient civilizations such as Egypt, Greece, and Rome, dancing was used in religious rituals, in training the young, and in developing artistic expression, as well as for pure enjoyment. Continuing through more recent eras, dancing has held a position of prominence up to the present time.

The records of the evolution of the dance are sketchy, and the exact origin of certain forms of dance is vague. For instance, when it comes to finding the origin of the American square dance one must do a considerable amount of speculating. The early dances and calls, except in rare cases, were never written, but were transmitted from caller to caller by word of mouth. Fortunately, through the efforts of a few, many of the bits and pieces about its origin have been put together.

Although square dancing is usually considered American, it stems from European folk dances that preceded it by several hundred years. The formation known as the "square" and most of the movements used in square dancing originated with the old European formation dances. Elements of the American square dance have been traced back to such diverse origins as the English Morris dance and the elegant ballroom dancing of the French aristocracy of the fifteenth century. Such European dances as the Scotch reels, Irish jigs, mazurka quadrilles, and the polka and waltz also have contributed to the American square dance.

Square dancing in America first developed along two separate lines, which resulted in the eastern square dance and the western (or cowboy) square dance. Even though the two were quite similar, each portrayed to a degree the personality and the way of life of its people.

The eastern dance was closely linked to New England country dances, such as the contra, the quadrille, and play-party dances, which were transplants from France and England.

Their traditionally formal influence carried through into the eastern square dance.

Although the western (or cowboy) dance also borrowed from the quadrille and the contra, it was more closely related to such Appalachian Mountain country dances as the big set and the Kentucky running set. It was also influenced by the Spanish and Mexican dances of the West and Southwest.

According to Lloyd Shaw, one of America's outstanding square-dance authorities, the two forms of dance that had the most direct influence on the square dance were the New England quadrilles and the Kentucky running set. In his book, *Cowboy Dances* (pp. 25-32), Shaw has compiled some interesting information about the relationship of these dances to the square dance.

THE NEW ENGLAND QUADRILLES

The New England or early American quadrilles were, of course, adaptations of European dances. Usually France is given credit for the origin of this form, although dances performed by four couples arranged in a square with a couple on each side of the square are found in the peasant dances of nearly all the European countries. Undoubtedly many of these contributed to the formal quadrilles which were finally perfected in France and England.

Unlike a square dance, in the quadrille the head couple is numbered one, the opposite couple two, the couple to the right three, and the couple to the left four. In the first figure, after an introduction, the opposite couples maneuver with each other in a variety of patterns across the set. In the other figures all four couples maneuver together around the square which becomes a circle of dancing action. Only occasionally does the first couple perform a maneuver with the right-hand couple then moves on to the opposite couple and finally to the couple on the left, thus working around the square. But this pattern of working around the set is a standard form of the square dance.

These New England quadrilles were so well known in early America that it is only natural they should be thought the chief source of the square dance. And they surely did contribute much, especially to the eastern form of dance. The singing quadrilles and similar dances in which the calls are sung, with words and music fixed, were especially influential on the eastern square dance. But as to its influence on the western dance, the quadrille is probably only a tributary; the main stream leading to its development was the Kentucky running set.

THE KENTUCKY RUNNING SET

In the mountains of Kentucky and throughout the Southern Appalachians, an old form of dance called the running set has survived. It is claimed as one of the purest and oldest dance forms of English origin. Some have erroneously thought of the running set as a rough, uncouth dance, remarkable only as an exhibition of agility and endurance. But this description is not valid because the dance has real aesthetic quality and much historic significance.

Observing the dance leads one to recognize immediately the source of much that is found in the western square dance. The calls and the spirit of the running set are much closer to the western form than is the New England Quadrille.

In the running set any number of dancers may join the figure, standing in couples in a circle. The dance can follow many patterns, but the following is a typical form. After an introductory "circle left," similar to the introduction of the western dance, the first couple moves to the second and performs a special figure, then to the next couple and repeats this figure. As they go on to the fourth couple, the second couple follows up and performs the same figure with the third couple, then follows behind the first couple and repeats the figure with each couple in the ring. As soon as possible, the third couple follows up and dances with the fourth, then follows around the ring. This goes on until every couple has followed in a sort of looping or crochet chain stitch of continuous and furious dancing. The figures the couples perform not only bear a resemblance to the western figures but in some cases are identical.

Even though any number of couples may participate in the running set, it is usually danced as a square with four couples. Shaw tells us (*Cowboy Dances*, pp. 29-30) that after a careful study of the running set, Cecil Sharp, one of England's best authorities on dance, concluded that the running set is the earliest known form of English country dance, earlier than any dance described in Playford's famous *English Dancing Master* (1650), the earliest known book on English dancing. The complete absence of courtesy movements is one bit of evidence for this conclusion.

RECENT DEVELOPMENTS

As our nation gradually became more mobile and methods of communication improved, influences of the East moved west, and those of the West spread eastward. The distinction between the two versions of square dance diminished until both merged into what is presently known as the American square dance.

Increasing urbanization in the United States brought sophistication to the traditional square dance with its strong rural flavor. City dancers, who became tired of this "country cousin" they had adopted, began shaping the dance to city standards. Much of the rustic-flavored patter, which seemed out of place in the new environment, was replaced by more dignified verses. Frontier phraseology gave way to phrases that had more meaning for urban dwellers.

Accompanying this urban influence on the patter was a growing demand for more activity during the dance. More figures were designed for all members of the set at once. As a result, the square dance became more complex and more strenuous. As new movements were added, callers began surprising the dancers with unexpected variations. They combined sections of memorized routines to form new dances. This spontaneous combining of parts from established routines became known as "hash." As the calling of hash became popular, the dancers could no longer memorize an entire dance; they had to listen carefully and dance whatever was called.

By this time the square dance movement was recruiting many new dancers who had little acquaintance with country dancing. In order to teach the dance techniques quickly, many callers organized courses of eight or ten weekly sessions. Square dance clubs held weekly dances, which became popular in cities and country towns alike. The square dance then was incorporated into school curricula at all levels, and many church organizations adopted the dance as a wholesome form of recreation.

Since its beginning the square dance has undergone almost constant change, and even today its movements and terminology are constantly changing. Because of this dynamic quality, square dancing continues to be challenging, interesting, and exciting even to the most experienced dancers.

3. Learn Positions for Square Dancing

FORMING THE SQUARE

As its name implies, the square dance (or square quadrille) is performed in a square formation composed of four couples. Each couple forms one side of the square.

When the dance begins, all couples face the center of the square, the ladies to the right of their partners. The set is squared (square the set) when partners stand shoulder to shoulder with outside arms extended to touch fingertips with the corresponding corner person (Figure 1). In this position the four couples form a nearly perfect square of the correct size.

Each couple in the set has a number in counterclockwise sequence. Couple number *one* is closest to but facing away from the music; couple *two* is on the right of couple one; couple *three* is opposite to and facing couple one; the remaining couple is number *four*. Because the women often change partners during the dance, they also change numbers. While a woman is dancing with man number two, she is the second lady. If she temporarily becomes the partner of man number

Figure 1

three, she becomes the third lady. In other words, the lady has the same number as the man with whom she is dancing.

Each couple is also designated as either a *head* couple or a *side* couple. One and three are head couples; two and four are side couples.

In the starting position, the lady on the man's right is his *partner*, and the one on his left is his *corner*. The one facing him is the *opposite* lady, and the one remaining is known as the *right-hand* lady, or the lady on the right.

STAR AND STAR PROMENADE FORMATIONS

The star formation may be assumed by any two or more dancers; however, it usually involves four, such as the four ladies, the four men, the head couples, or the side couples. When a right-hand star is formed, all of the dancers in the star face clockwise, extend the right arm to the center, and form a hub by grasping the wrist of the person in front (Figure 2) or by reaching high and to the center (Figure 3). The star rotates in the direction the dancers are facing unless the caller

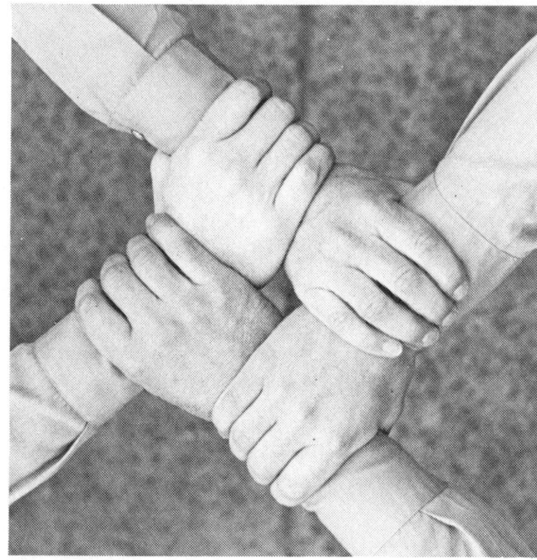

Figure 2

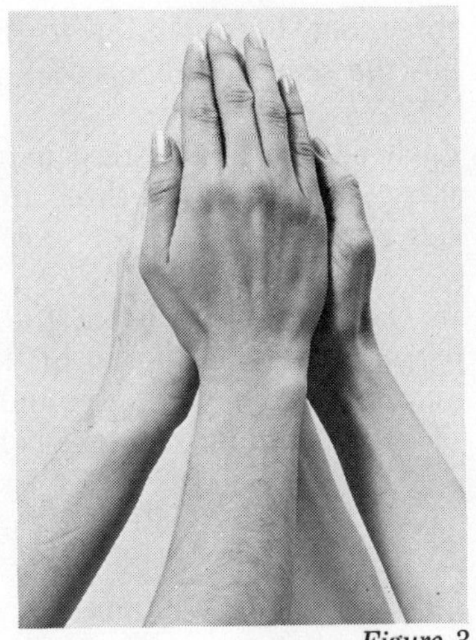

Figure 3

directs otherwise. To form a left-hand star, the dancers face counterclockwise and extend left hands to the center.

The star promenade formation (Figure 4) is the same as a four hand star, except that those in the star place their arms around their partners and take their partners along with them.

LINE FORMATION

Some square dance movements are done with the dancers formed in two lines of four facing each other (Figure 5). Some of the movements are done "down the line," while others are done "across the set."

Figure 5

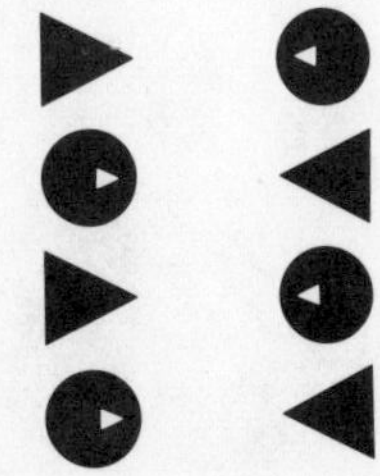

Figure 4

Figure 6

WAGON WHEEL

The wagon wheel is made up of the hub and the rim. The hub is composed of the four dancers on the inside (usually the men) who are in a four-hand star formation. The rim is made up of the partners of those forming the hub. Those on the rim face the opposite direction of their partners, and each couple holds inside hands.

COUPLE POSITIONS

The waist-swing position is the most common of the three swing positions. Two dancers stand with right hips close together and facing opposite directions. The man places his right arm around the lady's waist and holds her right hand in his left hand. The lady places her left hand on the man's right shoulder. Their right feet are kept close together to form a point of pivot around which the swing is performed in a clockwise direction as the dancers lean away from each other (Figure 6). The swing may be performed with a walking step or buzz step. If the walking step is used, very short steps are taken with the inside (right) foot, while longer steps are taken with the outside (left) foot in time with the music. The cadence should be even and the movements smooth. In the buzz step, the dancers rotate clockwise around the pivot formed by the right feet by pushing with the left feet in time with the music, a movement similar to pushing a child's scooter.

The elbow swing is done on either the right or left side, as designated by the caller. In the right-elbow-swing position, the two dancers again face opposite directions, with right sides close together. They hook right arms at the elbows and lean away from each other. The right feet remain fairly close together to form a hub. The dancers then rotate clockwise around the hub by walking in time with the music. (The buzz step may be used if desired.) The left-elbow position is performed in the same way, except that the partners have left sides together.

The arm-swing position is the same as the elbow position, except that the two dancers grasp the inside of each other's forearms near the elbow instead of hooking elbows.

The promenade position puts both dancers side by side, facing the same direction, the lady on the right. The couple join hands, with right hand in right, and left hand in left (Figure 7). The right hands are above the left hands.

Figure 7

The courtesy-turn position is the same as the promenade position except that the man's right arm passes behind the lady's waist, and he clasps her right hand, which is placed in a palm-up position on her right hip (Figure 8).

Figure 8

4. Learn Basic Movements

Learn Basic Movements

During its long evolution the square dance has adopted many new movements and discarded some old ones. But a number of the movements have held their popularity through the years. This chapter includes the most popular and basic movements used in contemporary square dancing. These movements are arranged in approximately the order in which they should be learned—that is, the simpler and more common movements first, as recommended by the American Square Dance Society. The Society refers to these movements as the fifty basics.

circle left and right
walk (shuffle)
forward and back
honors
do-sa-do
waist swing
couple promenade
single file promenade
square identification
split the ring—one couple
grand right and left/weave the ring
arm turns
couple separate
allemande left
bend the line
courtesy turn
ladies chain (two ladies)
do paso
right and left thru
ladies grand chain (four ladies chain)
right hand star
back by the left
star promenade
hub back out—rim turn in
circle to a line
all around left hand lady
see saw pretty little taw
promenade flourishes—twirls
pass thru

separate—go around one-two
grand square
frontier whirl (California twirl)
dive thru
around one to a line
ends turn in
cross trail
wheel around
box the gnat
single file turn back
allemande thar star
shoot that star
rollaway—half sashay
balance
alamo style
square thru
half promenade
star thru
couple backtrack
three-quarter chain
turn back

CIRCLE LEFT OR RIGHT

Three or more dancers can circle left or right as directed by the caller. As the men and ladies join hands, the men's palms should face upward and the ladies' palms downward. The hands should be held at slightly lower than shoulder height and slightly forward with the elbows partially bent.

WALK (SHUFFLE)

The walk is the gait mainly used in square dancing. The square dance walk is a comfortable, effortless shuffle done to the beat of the music. It should be done gracefully, demonstrating good posture and poise. The steps should be slightly shorter than normal, and the walk should be rhythmical. Often during the walk the men place their hands on the back portion of their hips with the palms turned backward, and the women hold their skirts slightly outward.

FORWARD AND BACK

Those individuals or couples designated by the caller move forward three steps, then back three steps. Count forward-two-three-touch, back-two-three-touch. The posture and styling which applies to the walk also applies to this movement.

HONORS

Honors is a movement calling for two people to acknowledge each other (Figure 9). It is performed by the man bowing and the lady curtsying. The man places his left hand (or both hands) in the small of his back, steps back on the left foot, shifts the weight to that foot and bends slightly forward at the hips. The lady steps back onto the right foot, pointing the left toe toward the man. She dips slightly by bending the legs but keeps the trunk and head erect. Simultaneously she spreads her skirts slightly sideward with the two hands.

Figure 9

DO—SA—DO

Two dancers face each other and advance forward until they pass right shoulders (Figure 10). Then each one moves to the right as they pass back to back. Without turning, they pass left shoulders as they move backward into their starting positions. This movement is sometimes written as dos-a-dos and is sometimes abbreviated as do-sa.

Figure 10

WAIST SWING

See the description of the waist swing in the previous chapter. The swing presents one of the best opportunities to add gracefulness and style to square dancing. It should consist of a smooth and flowing action, permitting the two dancers to keep their movements well coordinated with each other.

PROMENADE

Two dancers walk side by side in the promenade position and move counterclockwise (unless directed otherwise) around the set until they reach their home position. The promenade position is discussed and illustrated in the previous chapter.

SINGLE FILE PROMENADE

The dancers move one behind the other in a clockwise direction unless directed otherwise. To know the style of movement recommended, see the description of the walk, the second movement described in this chapter.

SQUARE IDENTIFICATION

The square, or set, with its various characteristics, is described in the previous chapter.

SPLIT THE RING

The active couple, having advanced forward, is commanded to split the ring. The couple passes between the couple facing them. For example, if couple one were commanded to split the ring, they would advance forward, then pass between the opposite couple (couple three). Unless otherwise directed, the lady would then turn to her right and the man to his left, and they would continue around the outside of the set.

GRAND RIGHT AND LEFT/WEAVE THE RING

In a square or circle formation facing each other join right hands and move forward, passing right shoulders (men counter-clockwise and ladies clockwise). Each person then gives a left hand to the next, a right to the next, a left to the next and so on until each dancer meets his partner and is then ready to follow the next call.

Weave the ring (Figure 11) is the same as a grand right and left, except that the dancers do not join hands. Men should place their hands behind their backs, and ladies should wave their skirts as they weave in and out.

Figure 11

ARM TURNS

The two dancers facing each other assume a forearm hold, with the hand of each person placed just below and inside the elbow of the other person. The two walk around each other in a clockwise direction. The center of the turn (point of pivot) should be halfway between the hands of the two dancers.

COUPLES SEPARATE

Sometimes the caller will tell two dancers to separate. The couple turn their backs on each other, then follow the directions of the next call. Usually the dancers are told to promenade around the outside of the square. When they meet on the other side, the man should pass on the outside while the lady stays closest to the square. All those not active should "close ranks" so the active couple will not have so far to go.

ALLEMANDE LEFT

Two dancers facing each other join left hands (right hands for an allemande right), walk around each other, and move back to starting position. This movement is usually performed with the corner person, and it is commonly followed by a grand right and left.

BEND THE LINE

The dancers begin in a line-of-four formation (see description of formation in previous chapter), usually facing outward.

Figure 12

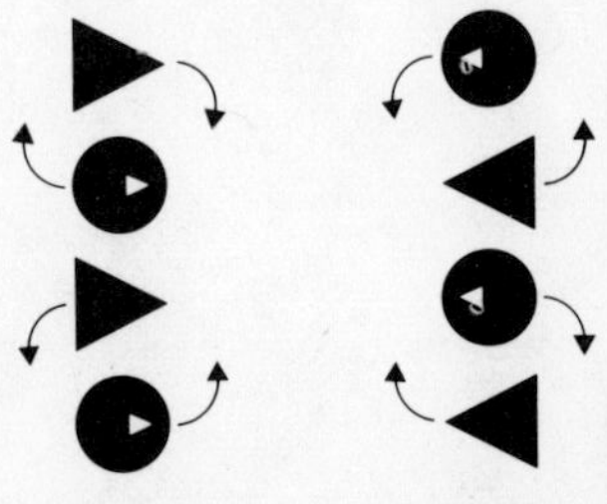

They break the line in the middle, and the ends move forward while the centers move backward until both halves are facing each other (Figure 12). After the line is broken the point of pivot for each couple is the same as described under "arm turns."

COURTESY TURN

The courtesy turn is used as an ending for several movements, including ladies' chain, grand chain, right and left thru, and do paso. To perform the movement, the lady moves toward the man, and they join left hands. The man then does a half left turn so that he stands beside the lady, both facing the same direction. The man places his right arm around the lady's waist in the courtesy-turn position (see previous chapter), and the couple wheel halfway around.

TWO LADIES CHAIN

The two active ladies advance, join right hands, walk past each other (Figure 13), join left hands with the opposite men and the men courtesy turn the ladies.

Figure 13

DO PASO

Beginning from a circle of two or more couples, each dancer faces his partner and assumes the left forearm position with that person. After turning counterclockwise completely, each dancer goes to the corner, assumes the right forearm position, and turns clockwise completely around. Each person then returns to his starting partner and does a courtesy turn in place. Actually a do paso can start from positions other than a circle. But ordinarily the circle is the beginning formation for this movement.

RIGHT AND LEFT THRU

The two active couples move toward each other, join right hands with the opposite person, and pass right shoulders (Figure 14). Partners then join left hands and the man courtesy turns the lady. The two couples complete the movement in positions opposite from where they started.

Figure 14

FOUR LADIES CHAIN (GRAND CHAIN)

The four ladies form a right-hand star and rotate clockwise, half way around. Then each lady joins left hands with the man opposite her, and he courtesy turns her.

RIGHT HAND (LEFT HAND) STAR

This movement is usually performed by four people, such as the four men, the four ladies, the head couples, or the side couples. Those called to perform the star advance to the center of the square. Each dancer extends his right hand to the center and joins hands with the other three dancers in the star (see illustration of the star in the previous chapter). The dancers then rotate the direction they are facing.

BACK BY THE LEFT

From a right-hand star position, the dancers change to a left-hand star. Those involved release the right-hand hold, make a half turn to the right (turning in) and form a left-hand star, then move forward counterclockwise.

The movement "ladies to the center, back to the bar" is a companion movement that often precedes the star movements. On this call the ladies move from their home positions three steps toward the center of the square then three steps back to their home positions.

STAR PROMENADE

The four men go into a left-hand star, then place their right arms around the waists of their partners. Each lady places her left arm around the waist of her partner or on his right shoulder. The couples are now side by side, and the men are in a left-hand star. The star rotates counterclockwise, the direction the dancers are facing. (See the illustration of the star promenade in the previous chapter.)

HUB BACK OUT—RIM TURN IN (INSIDE OUT—OUTSIDE IN)

From a star promenade position the couples keep hold of each other while the centers (those forming the star) back out and those on the outside move forward into the center and form a star. This results in a star promenade position with the ladies on the inside forming a right-hand star. The star then rotates clockwise.

CIRCLE TO A LINE

With two couples forming a ring and circling to the left, the man indicated by the caller breaks the hold with his left hand while retaining the hold with his right hand. All others in the circle retain their hand holds, and the four dancers spread out to form a line of four, facing toward the center of the set.

ALL AROUND YOUR LEFT HAND LADY

This movement is very similar to a do-sa-do with the corner, except the two dancers do not pass back to back. While the man moves forward and around his corner in a clockwise loop, the lady, having faced the man, moves forward in a clockwise loop around him. The two dancers keep their right shoulders adjacent during the movement.

SEE SAW YOUR PRETTY LITTLE TAW

This is a companion movement to "all around your left hand lady," and the two movements are performed the same way, except that in the see saw the two dancers go around each other in the counterclockwise direction whereas in the previous movement they go around in the clockwise direction. In the see saw the left shoulders are kept adjacent to each other.

PROMENADE FLOURISHES—TWIRLS

In non-exhibition square dancing (recreational dancing) the twirl is used only to precede a promenade or in some cases to close a promenade. (See the section on styling in chapter 6.) For a pick-up twirl to a promenade following a right and left grand, the joined right hands of the two dancers are held high, and the lady does a right face turn one and a half times under the man's right hand. At the completion of the turn, the right hands are lowered and the left hands are joined to form a promenade position. At the end of the promenade the right hands are raised once again, and the lady does a half turn clockwise under the man's right arm as the two dancers move away from each other into a balance position (also in the section on styling in chapter 6).

PASS THRU

Two couples facing each other advance forward, each person passing right shoulders with the person facing him (Figure 15). One couple moves to the position vacated by the other couple. They remain facing outward until the next call is given.

Figure 15

SEPARATE—GO AROUND ONE—TWO

This movement is done by two couples having done a pass thru or by one couple after splitting the ring. When the couples are told to separate, they turn their backs on each other and move around the set in opposite directions. They continue until they have passed behind the number of dancers designated by the caller.

GRAND SQUARE

The head couples and side couples perform the movement in different directions at the same time (Figure 16). On the command "grand square," the head couples move forward four steps toward the center. Each person then does a quarter turn to face his partner. The dancers back away from their partners four steps, then do a quarter turn to face their opposites. The dancers back away another four steps and do a quarter turn to face their partners. The couples advance four steps until they meet their partners face to face. While the

Figure 16

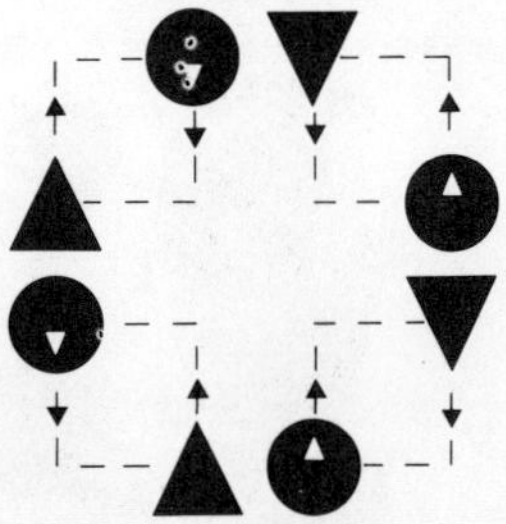

head couples are performing the movement just described, the side couples simultaneously perform the same movement in the opposite direction. In other words, on the command "grand square" the side couples face each other and back away four steps. Then each person does a quarter turn to face his opposite and advances forward four steps. Then each person does a quarter turn to face his partner, and advances forward another four steps. Each one does a quarter turn to face his opposite, and the couples back away four steps, into their starting position. When the command "reverse" is given, each dancer begins the movement in the opposite direction from his original grand square.

FRONTIER WHIRL (CALIFORNIA TWIRL)

The two dancers, side by side with the lady on the right, join inside hands. They then do a facing movement toward each other as they exchange places, the lady walking under the raised right arm of the man and the man walking around the outside of the lady. The two dancers have then exchanged positions and also reversed directions.

DIVE THRU

With two couples facing each other, the couple whose back is to the center of the square (unless otherwise indicated) makes an arch with inside hands joined. The other couple duck under the arch while moving forward. The couple making the arch also moves forward and then, at the completion of the movement, automatically does a frontier whirl (California twirl) to face back toward the center of the square.

AROUND ONE TO A LINE

After splitting a couple, the active dancers separate, and each one moves in his or her direction around an inactive dancer and steps up beside that dancer to form a line of four with the inactive couple in the center.

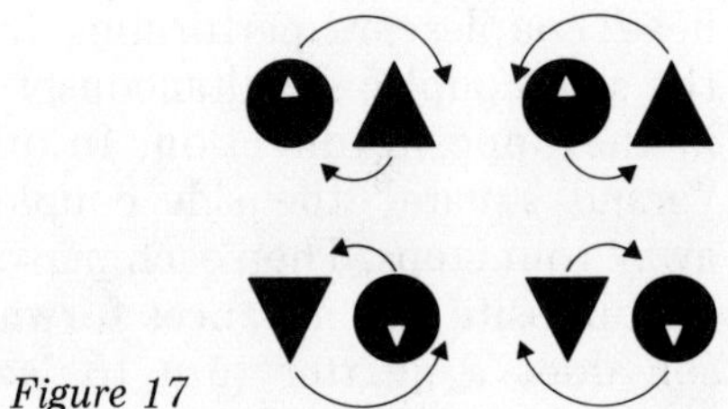

Figure 17

ENDS TURN IN

The dancers are in a line-of-four formation facing outward from the center of the set. The two dancers in the middle form an arch by joining inside hands and holding them high. The two on the ends step forward, perform a half-facing movement and dive under the arch (Figure 17). The two who formed the arch then perform a frontier whirl (California twirl) in order to reverse their direction and face the center of the set.

CROSS TRAIL

This is the same as the pass thru except that after each person passes right shoulders with the one facing him, each man turns diagonally to the right and crosses behind his partner, who advances diagonally to the left. The movement ends with the couples facing away from the center, the lady on the left of her partner.

WHEEL AROUND

While in a couple promenade position, the pair of dancers reverse direction by the man backing up and the lady walking forward a half turn. The pivot point is the spot between the two dancers. The turn results in an about-face, causing the man to be on the outside and the woman on the inside of the square.

Figure 18

BOX THE GNAT

Partners face each other and join right hands. They advance toward each other, and the lady passes under the man's raised right arm as she performs a half left-facing movement (Figure 18). At the same time, the man performs a half right-facing movement. At the completion of the movement, the dancers have exchanged positions and reversed directions.

SINGLE FILE TURN BACK

From a single file promenade formation those indicated by the caller do a half turn outward and promenade outside the set in the opposite direction. Those not indicated by the caller continue in their original direction of movement.

Figure 19

ALLEMANDE THAR STAR

The men move into a right-hand-star position and assume a left-forearm grip with their partners. The men, now on the inside in a right-hand star, are facing clockwise. The ladies, on the rim (outside), are facing counterclockwise. Partners have left arms joined (Figure 19). The star rotates in a counterclockwise direction, men moving backward. The men could be on the outside (rim) and the ladies in the star, if so indicated by the caller.

SHOOT THE STAR

This movement is used to shift out of the allemande thar formation. On the command "shoot the star," the four men break their right-hand star but maintain the left-forearm grips with their partners. Each couple does a half turn in a counterclockwise direction. The dancers are then ready for the next call.

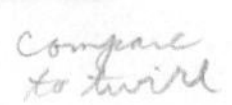

ROLLAWAY WITH A HALF SASHAY

With partners standing side by side facing the same direction and holding inside hands, the lady rolls across in front of the man doing a full turn. The man steps slightly sideways toward the position the lady has vacated. The two are now on opposite sides of each other and holding opposite hands.

BALANCE

The balance may be performed in either of the following two styles: (a) Partners face each other, join right hands, take one step forward, close or touch with the other foot, then step back and touch or close. (This is the movement that would be done unless directed otherwise.) (b) Partners face each other, join right hands, step with the right foot and swing the left foot in front, then step with the left foot and swing the right foot in front.

ALAMO STYLE

This is a balance-type movement performed in a circle formation with dancers facing alternate directions and hands joined. In time to the music, each dancer balances forward two counts in the direction he is facing, then back two counts. The dancers then let go with left hands, but maintain holds with right hands. Each couple performs a half turn clockwise. Dancers join hands again and repeat the balance forward and balance back. Then the dancers break with the right hands but maintain holds with the left hands. Each couple then performs a half turn counterclockwise. The movement continues until the next call is given.

SQUARE THRU

Two couples facing each other advance to the center of the set and join right hands with their opposites. The dancers pass right shoulders with those facing them, and each person immediately does a quarter facing movement and joins left hands with his partner. Partners then pass left shoulders. (A half square thru has been completed at this point.) Each couple then performs another facing movement to face the opposite couple again. Each dancer joins right hands and passes right shoulders with his opposite. (A three-quarter square thru has been completed at this point.) The couples then perform another facing movement to join left hands with partners and advance forward, passing left shoulders (Figure 20). The square thru is completed at this point. If the

Figure 20

Figure 21

caller calls "square thru six hands 'round," the dancers will continue the movement for another half square thru. In other words, six hands 'round would be one and one-half square thrus. The caller may also call "square thru five hands 'round," or any other number of hands.

HALF PROMENADE (PROMENADE HALF)

Two couples facing each other exchange places by promenading counterclockwise past each other, then occupying the position vacated by the other couple. If opposite couples in the square half promenade, they will promenade halfway around the inside of the square. Sometimes couples are directed by the caller to half promenade on the outside of the square, but they would do this only when specifically directed.

STAR THRU

The two dancers face each other and join hands, with the man's right and the lady's left. They progress toward each other as the lady passes under the man's raised right arm (Figure 21). As the lady passes under, she performs a quarter left turn. The man passes around the outside of the lady and performs a quarter right turn. The two dancers finish the movement standing side by side, with the lady on the right of the man.

COUPLE BACKTRACK

From the promenade position the man and lady each do individual about-face turns while retaining hand holds. They turn toward each other, with the man right and the lady left. The couple is now facing opposite its original direction, with the man still on the inside and the lady on the outside.

THREE-QUARTER CHAIN

This movement is similar to a two-ladies chain or four-ladies chain except the ladies rotate three-quarters instead of one-half. The ladies designated form a right-hand star in the center of the square and walk forward three-quarters around, where each lady meets her corner man. Each lady joins left hands with her corner, and he courtesy turns her.

TURN BACK

At the completion of a grand right and left, instead of promenading, partners join right forearms and turn halfway around to face the opposite direction. Then they do a right and left grand in the opposite direction unless directed otherwise by the caller.

5. Discover Additional Movements

Discover Additional Movements

After the basic movements described in chapter four have been mastered, a number of additional movements should be learned. This chapter contains descriptions of the additional movements, used less frequently than the basic movements, but still commonly used in square dancing today. The first twenty-five movements included in this chapter have been identified by the American Square Dance Society as the extended basics. (The fifty movements in the previous chapter are the basics.) The twenty-five extended basics are arranged in the order recommended by the Society. The additional movements beyond the first twenty-five are movements not included in the Society's list.

turn thru
wrong way thar
slip the clutch (throw in the clutch)
eight chain thru
ocean wave
swing thru
circulate
run
trade
spin the top
trade by
wheel and deal
double pass thru
centers in
cast off
cloverleaf
slide thru
fold
Dixie chain
substitute
Dixie style
spin chain thru
peel off
pass to the center
tag the line
sashay
box the flea
all eight chain
catch all eight
red hot
sashay thru
split circulate
circle to a two-faced line
turn and left thru
rip and snort
slide thru
left square thru
daisy chain
barge thru
hinge and trade
curlique
scoot back

TURN THRU

This movement is done by a dance couple. Facing each other, they join right forearms and turn clockwise one-half turn. After exchanging places they move directly forward, passing right shoulders, releasing arm holds, and completing the movement back to back with each other. Remember in arm-hold turns the point of pivot should be halfway between the two dancers.

WRONG WAY THAR

Following a hand or forearm-couple turn, a wrong way thar may be formed. The men (or the women, if so directed) hold onto the women (or men) which they have just turned and move into a left-hand star. The dancers are now in the same formation as in an allemande thar except that they are facing the opposite direction.

SLIP THE CLUTCH (THROW IN THE CLUTCH)

From an allemande thar or a wrong way thar formation, those in the center retain the star position but release arm grips with their partners on the rim. The men in the star then change directions while the ladies continue to walk forward. This movement continues until the next call is given.

EIGHT CHAIN THRU

Each dancer joins right hands with the person designated, moves past that person, and joins left hands with the next dancer (Figure 22). Each couple then performs a courtesy turn to face the center of the set.

OCEAN WAVE

This movement is usually preceded by a call such as "do-sa-do, all the way 'round to an ocean wave." The dancers are in a line formation facing alternate directions with hands joined and the ladies in the center of the line. Each dancer then

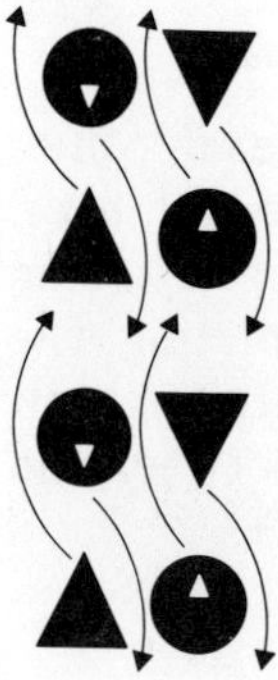

Figure 22

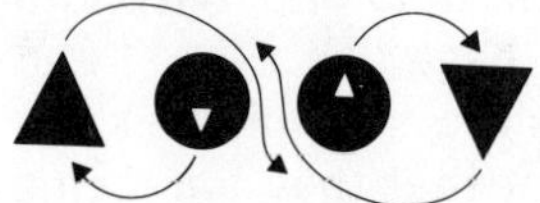

Figure 23

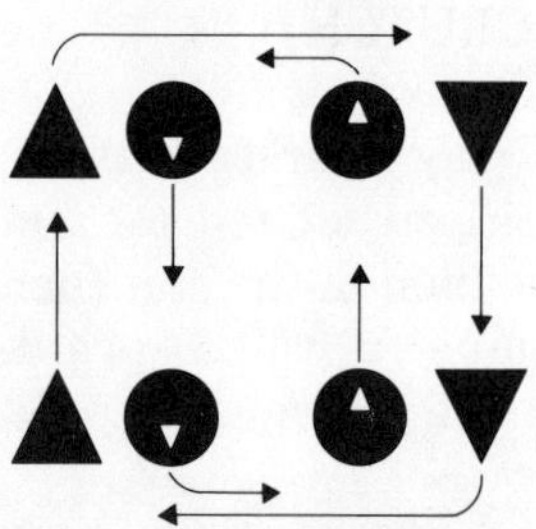

Figure 24

steps forward onto the left foot (two counts), then back onto the right foot (two counts).

SWING THRU

This is usually done from an ocean-wave line (line of four with dancers facing alternate directions). On the call "swing thru," the ends swing half way around with the adjacent dancers. The new center two then join hands and swing half way around to make a new ocean-wave line (Figure 23). If at the beginning the men were on the ends of the line, they are now in the center.

CIRCULATE

The movement starts with the dancers in two lines of four and those within each line facing alternate directions (ocean-wave line). On the command "circulate," the four dancers (usually the men) on the ends of the lines rotate one position in a clockwise direction. At the same time, the four dancers on the inside rotate one position in the counterclockwise direction (Figure 24). The call may be for only the center dancers to circulate, in which case the outside dancers remain stationary. Or the call may be for only the ends to circulate, in which case the centers remain stationary.

RUN

This movement is done from a line of four with the dancers facing alternating directions as in an ocean wave. Either the center two or the end two in the line can be directed to "run." If the centers are directed to run, the two people in the center of the line walk around the two people on the ends of the line, doing a 180-degree turn. The ends move in to occupy the vacancies left by the centers; thus the center two become the new ends of the line. Two couples are now standing side by side, facing opposite directions. When the ends are directed to run, they walk halfway around the centers while the centers move out to allow space for the ends to move in.

TRADE

From any line formation where the dancers are not facing within the line, those dancers designated by the caller (men, ladies, heads, sides, ends, centers, etc.) will trade places in the same line by walking forward and around a half circle, passing right shoulders, and taking the place of the other person (Figure 25). Each active dancer ends up facing the opposite direction from where he started, and he occupies the space vacated by the other active person.

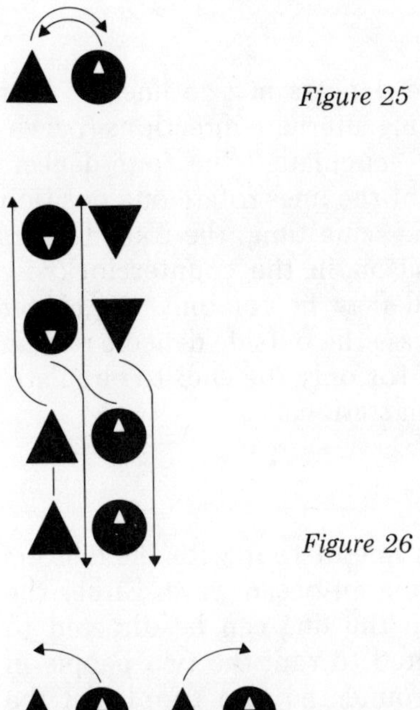

Figure 25

Figure 26

Figure 27

SPIN THE TOP

From a line of four people facing alternate directions, such as in an ocean wave formation, the two in the center break holds with each other, and the two couples holding hands turn halfway around. The new center two then take a hand hold and turn in a forward direction three-quarters around. While the center two are turning, the end dancers move forward one-quarter of the way around and join the inside two in another ocean wave formation of four in a line. The line is now at right angles to the original formation.

TRADE BY

This movement is started from an eight-chain-thru position where the center four are facing inward and the end four are facing outward. On the command "trade by," those facing inward pass through while those facing outward trade.

WHEEL AND DEAL

Two couples are in a line of four, facing outward. The right-hand couple does a half-turning movement with the inside person holding the pivot. At the same time the left-hand couple advances forward and does a right half-turning movement into a position directly behind the other couple. The right-hand couple always wheels into a position in front of the left-hand couple.

DOUBLE PASS THRU

With four couples lined up as they would be at the end of a wheel-and-deal movement, all four couples advance forward, passing right shoulders with the dancers facing them (Figure 26). This continues until each couple passes through two other couples.

CENTERS IN

With two couples facing the same direction and one couple directly behind the other, the lead couple steps apart, and the couple coming from behind moves between, resulting in a line of four with all four people facing the same direction.

CAST OFF

Two couples are in a line of four and holding hands. (Usually men are paired with men and women with women for this movement.) The two center dancers break, and both couples perform a turning movement away from each other (Figure 27). The two outside dancers pivot while their partners (inside dancers) circle around the outside of the pivot.

CLOVERLEAF

From a completed double-pass-thru formation, the two outside couples step forward slightly and separate, and each one moves one-quarter of the way around the outside of the square until he makes contact with another dancer coming toward him. The two people who meet then turn to face the square and step forward toward the center. Those couples second in line in the formation simply follow the couples in front of them by first moving forward, then dividing and moving one-quarter of the way around the square until each one meets another person coming toward him. The couple who meet face directly behind the other couple to end in a double-pass-thru formation which is at right angles to the original double-pass-thru formation.

SLIDE THRU

Two dancers facing each other move forward, passing right shoulders. Each will then turn one-quarter with the man always turning right and the lady always turning left. The figure starts with two dancers facing each other and ends with the same two dancers standing side by side.

FOLD

The folding movement is done either with a single couple or with a line of four. With a couple either the man or lady can be directed to fold. The one directed to fold simply walks around in a half arc and faces the other person (Figure 28). (Fold a lady: the lady moves around; fold a man: the man moves around.) From a line-of-four formation, either the ends might be directed to fold, or the centers might be directed to fold or either the men or the ladies might be directed to fold. In any of these cases those directed to fold walk around and face the dancers standing next to them.

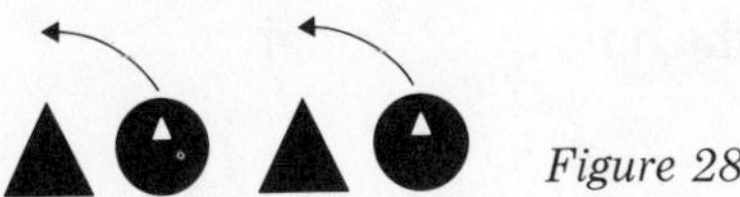

Figure 28

Figure 29a

Figure 29b

DIXIE CHAIN

Two couples are facing each other in a single-line formation, with the ladies standing in front of their partners. The couples advance toward each other and perform a movement similar to the right and left grand (Figure 29a, 29b). The two ladies join right hands and pass right shoulders; then they join left hands with the men facing them and pass left shoulders. Then the two men join right hands and pass right shoulders. The couples complete the movement, still in single-file.

SUBSTITUTE

Two couples, one behind the other, are facing the center of the set. The couple in front forms an arch and begins moving backward. The couple behind dives under the arch toward the center of the set. The couple forming the arch usually shifts to an inactive role, and the couple diving under becomes the active couple.

DIXIE STYLE

This movement starts like a Dixie chain but does not complete the chain. The starting movement of a Dixie style is the same as for a Dixie chain—that is, two couples facing in single file. Those in the lead join right hands and pull each other by, then left hand to the next, and all pull by. Retaining left holds, the two who are now in the center take right hands, and all four individuals adjust slightly to face in alternating directions in an ocean wave formation.

SPIN CHAIN THRU

With four couples arranged in two parallel ocean wave formations, those in the centers release hand holds with each other, and all four couples turn about their joined hands halfway around. Then the two in the center of each ocean wave turn three-quarters around to make an ocean wave across the set. Without stopping, the two in the center of this new wave turn halfway around to form the wave across the set once more. Still without stopping the ocean wave breaks in the middle, and the two pairs turn three-quarters to finish in two similar parallel ocean waves.

PEEL OFF

From a formation where one couple is directly behind another, both facing in the same direction, the lead couple moves forward slightly, separates, and the dancers make individual 180-degree turns to face the opposite direction and to form the ends of a line with the couple behind forming the

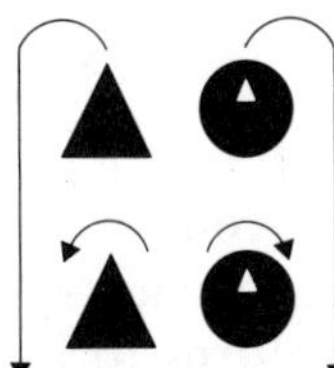

Figure 30

center of the line (Figure 30). At the same time the couple behind steps forward between the split couple and the second couple separates to make a tight 180-degree turn to assume their positions in the center of the line with both couples now facing the same direction in a line of four.

PASS TO THE CENTER

Beginning with an eight-chain-thru formation, all dancers will pass through. Those now on the outside of the square do a partner trade while those in the center stand ready to react to the next call. When starting from a two-parallel ocean wave formation, those facing out from the center of the square release hand holds, move forward, and do a partner trade. Those facing toward the center of the square move forward to follow the next call.

TAG THE LINE

From any line of four, six, or eight dancers in any facing direction or combination of facing directions, the dancers turn to face the center point in the line. After taking a short side step to their left, the dancers move forward, passing right shoulders with the dancers facing the other direction. At this time they will be given the follow-up command which will tell them which direction to turn individually. After having passed the dancers facing the opposite direction, each dancer will turn in the direction specified by the caller to end in two equal lines facing each other.

SASHAY

Partners stand side by side, lady on the right. Still facing the center of the square, the lady moves to her left in front of the man as he moves to his right behind her. The lady then steps back as the man steps forward, and the man returns to his starting position by passing in front of the lady as she passes behind him. Both are now back to their starting positions. Originally this movement was performed in a series of sliding steps. Today, walking steps are more common.

BOX THE FLEA

This is performed the same as box the gnat, except that the partners join left hands rather than right hands, and the lady does a half right-facing movement as she passes under the man's left arm.

ALL EIGHT CHAIN

Each dancer joins right hands with the person designated, and moves past that person and joins left hands with the next dancer. Each couple then performs a courtesy turn to face the center of the set.

CATCH ALL EIGHT

Couples face each other and assume the right-forearm grip. The couples first swing in the direction they are facing for only two steps, then each person does a quick half-facing movement as he changes to a left-forearm grip. The couples then perform a counterclockwise turning movement for four or more steps as directed by the caller.

RED HOT

This movement is usually started from a promenade position. Each lady does a half left-facing movement as she moves in front of her partner. Each man moves to his right-hand lady and turns her half around with a right-forearm swing. Then he returns to his partner, and they perform a complete turn with the left-forearm swing. The man then moves to his corner lady and does a right-forearm swing half around, and then returns to his partner for another complete left-forearm swing.

SASHAY THRU

Beginning with two couples facing each other, each dancer starts a do-sa-do with the person facing him. After the do-sa-do is three-quarters completed, the two in the center slide past each other to the right (nose-to-nose) and each person finishes the movement standing next to his original partner.

SPLIT CIRCULATE

Beginning from an ocean wave position, each dancer circulates one position in the box of four people, formed by an imaginary divider which goes across both waves, splitting the waves into boxes of four.

CIRCLE TO A TWO-FACED LINE

Starting from a square formation, those couples designated lead to the right and circle exactly one-half. Then the circle breaks, and each couple side-steps left, then moves forward slightly to form a two-faced line. At the completion of the movement, the set is formed into two two-faced lines.

TURN AND LEFT THRU

Beginning with two couples facing each other, the couples do a turn thru and at the completion of the turn thru the left-hand person courtesy turns the right-hand person to end in the starting position.

RIP AND SNORT

All join hands and circle. The designated couple walks down the center of the set, hands still joined, passing under the joined hands of the opposite couple. The designated couple break hand holds with each other, and the lady moves to her right and the man to his left. They continue, leaving the other dancers behind them, until they return to their home position, thus turning the circle inside out. The couple who made the arch continue to hold hands, and the man makes a right face turn while the lady makes a left face turn under their own joined hands, and the circle is once again complete.

SLIDE THRU

The same as the star thru except that no hand turns are involved. The dancers merely move into the positions described in the star thru.

LEFT SQUARE THRU

The same as a square thru except it starts with the left hand instead of the right.

DAISY CHAIN

This is similar to a grand right and left. The dancers, however, progress forward with a right and a left and then turn back to make a hand turn with the person behind them, then forward again with two hands and back one, thus progressing around the set until the original partner is met, or until the caller terminates the movement. Two couples facing each other walk forward and turn the opposite person one-quarter. All are now facing their partners. Moving down the line, each person turns his partner with a left hand, continuing all the way around so that all dancers face in the direction from which they started. The dancers now turn the opposite person one-quarter with the right hand, then the partner again with the left hand, continuing all the way around until partners are in original positions.

BARGE THRU

Beginning from two lines of four facing each other, the two lines approach each other, and all dancers do a half square thru (two hands). Then those facing inward do a pass thru while those facing outward do a partner trade. The movement ends in an eight-chain-thru formation.

HINGE AND TRADE

Starting in two lines of four facing outward, everyone goes half way through a wheel and deal movement. At this point the left hand persons of the center two couples hook arms, do a couples trade, and then bend the line, while at the same time the outside couples complete the wheel and deal. The movement ends in a double pass-thru formation.

CURLIQUE

A man and woman face each other, join right hands, and the hands are raised. The man then does the equivalent of a star thru while the woman does a three-fourths left-face twirl under the man's arm. The movement ends with the right shoulders close together.

SCOOT BACK

The movement starts from two parallel ocean waves. Those facing outward fold into the spot of those that were facing in. Simultaneously those facing inward walk forward and turn the opposite person one-half by the inside arm then walk straight ahead into the vacant place. The movement ends in a parallel ocean wave formation.

6. Improve Dancing Techniques

To gain the fullest enjoyment from square dancing, you must do more than learn the movements. The greatest pleasure comes from performing well. Therefore, in addition to learning the basic movements, you should concentrate on: (1) bodily posture and movement, (2) improving rhythm and gracefulness, (3) following the calls, (4) adding extra movements, and (5) following basic rules of conduct.

BODILY POSTURE AND MOVEMENT

The basic footwork for beginners should be a shuffle-type walking step, smooth and gliding, timed to the music. After dancers are experienced, they can use the two-step or other more difficult step patterns. But first the dancers should become well acquainted with the basic dance movements.

As in other forms of dance, posture is important. Good posture adds gracefulness and dignity to the dancer and beauty to the dance itself. The square dancer's posture should be relaxed enough for graceful and easy movements, but slouchy and careless posture should be strictly avoided.

IMPROVING RHYTHM AND GRACEFULNESS

Almost all square-dance music is written to either 2/4 or 4/4 meter (time). This means that a dancer takes two steps during each measure of the music. Frequently, those with little experience in dancing or music find it difficult to recognize the basic beat and to move accurately to the specific count of the music. Although a certain amount of rhythmic aptitude may be inherited, one should realize that such aptitude can, to a large measure, be developed through practice. Dancing is probably the best method for improving rhythm, but other approaches also help. Here are some suggestions:

1. Listen frequently to music. As you do this, clap your hands or tap one foot in time with the music.

2. While listening to the music, count the beat aloud.

3. Walk in time to the music, matching your steps with the accented beats.

4. Whenever you hear music, consciously concentrate on hearing the beat and moving in time to the music.

After you have developed your sense of rhythm, concentrate on making your movements smooth and graceful. In beginning square dance the only foot patterns involved are the walking step and the step used in swinging, which may be a walking step or a buzz step. In the walking step, the dancer takes two steps to each measure of music. The following instructions will help you achieve graceful walking steps:

1. Keep the feet close together and the body in good alinement. Do not waddle from side to side.

2. Hold your body erect, but not rigid, and balance your weight forward so that each step is led by forward movement at the hip.

3. Keep the feet close to the floor and use a gliding step. Transfer your weight smoothly from one foot to the other.

4. If you are on the inside when walking in couple position around the square, remember to shorten your steps so that the outside person (usually the lady) need not take exaggerated steps.

FOLLOWING THE CALLS

Square dancing is unique in that the dancers do not choose the patterns they dance. Nor does the music give them cues, as in some dance routines. In square dancing the caller selects the patterns and calls them to the dancers, who attempt to perform the movements as they are called. Therefore, it is imperative for the dancers to listen carefully and execute the movements promptly—or they will lag behind the caller. Square dancing is, then, a challenge to a dancer's alertness and his ability to perform gracefully.

Square dancing has its own terminology which dancers must understand in order to follow the calls. The previous chapter contains descriptions of the most popular movements. Additional terms encountered in the dance are listed in the glossary.

ADDING EXTRA MOVEMENTS

Extra movements are those not commanded by the caller that may add grace and pleasure to the dance. Try some of these after you have learned to perform the basic movements gracefully and in time to the music. Following are some suggestions:

1. As dancers move from the right and left grand into the promenade, the man may twirl the lady into promenade position. At the completion of the right-and-left-grand movement, the couples have right hands joined. The man raises his right hand and pulls it slightly to the left turning the lady toward him and under his right arm. The lady performs a one and one-half clockwise turning movement into a promenade position.

2. When the couples arrive at their home stations after doing a promenade, the man may twirl the girl into a balance-away position followed by a swing. At the completion of the promenade, the couples maintain the right-hand hold. The man raises his right hand high, and leads the lady under the raised right arm as she executes a half turning movement in a clockwise direction. The two dancers then balance away from each other with arms extended and holding right hands. The balance may be followed by a swing if time permits.

3. Often dancers find themselves with a few seconds to spare while waiting for the next command call. This time may be well used in swinging. Extra swinging adds to the pleasure of dancing and to the beauty of the dance.

4. Rather than performing the regular promenade, in exhibition dancing, you may wish to do the twirling promenade. From a promenade position the dancers release left hands.

While holding right hands, they raise the right hands high, and the lady performs a series of clockwise twirls directly underneath the man's right arm. The movement continues until the promenade is completed.

5. Some exhibition dancers enjoy doing a spinning or turning movement into an allemande left. Instead of simply advancing toward the corner, the dancers do an individual counterclockwise turn before joining left hands. The allemande left is then completed as usual.

THE BASIC RULES OF CONDUCT 

The rules of conduct for square dancing are based on consideration, courtesy, and dancing efficiency. Every dancer should know the rules and practice them consistently.

1. Listen carefully to the calls. Forget the mistake you just made and think of what is coming next; otherwise, you will make another mistake. Think of the caller as the quarterback. He gives the signals; you execute the movements as he calls them.

2. Practice social etiquette. Although the history of square dancing is associated with the rugged western frontier, many changes have occurred in square dancing since the west was won. Now, etiquette is just as important at a square dance as at any social occasion.

3. Be a thoughtful dancer. Personal cleanliness is important in any activity where people exercise vigorously in close contact with each other; almost everyone needs a good deodorant and mouth wash. Because the success of the dance depends upon neuromuscular coordination, alcoholic beverages have no place in square dancing.

4. Be cooperative. The greatest pleasure in square dancing comes when each person does his share to help the set function smoothly. Do not try to steal the show, but contribute your part as one of eight members of the set.

5. Dance gracefully and smoothly. Skipping, jumping, and other jerky movements do not belong in square dancing.

6. Take your share of the blame. It usually takes two people to make one mistake. In any event, it is discourteous to blame others.

7. Be helpful. Help those who have less dancing background than you. Be courteous as you assist them through the dance.

8. Be a good mixer. This means do not form cliques; do not avoid entering sets because of certain people in them; and after entering a set, never leave that set until the dance tip is over.

9. Enjoy yourself. The whole purpose of square dancing is to have fun with others. Enter into the spirit of the activity. At the same time, be careful not to impose upon the pleasure of others. Be moderate in such things as clapping, yelling, and swinging which may accompany having a good time.

STYLING

Styling is just as important in square dancing as it is in other forms of dance. It should be taught along with the fundamentals of square dancing. Following are some important guides.

1. Teach "anti-roughness" right from the start. For example, a man should not twirl a girl. He should offer support as she twirls herself under his upraised arm. In an arm turn the woman should not be "shoved around" as the man remains in place, but both should move equally around their joined arms.

2. Nothing is more unsatisfactory than dancing with a "dead fish." For example, to do an allemande left with a person who offers no resistance or to swing with a dancer who instead of counterbalancing simply gives way is highly unsatisfying. Without being rough and overly vigorous, dancers will

discover that regardless of their own stature or weight they can counterbalance the person with whom they are dancing.

3. Do not forget that the activity is "square dancing" and not "square standing." When not active, a dancer should not stand motionless in place like some bit of statuary but should move slightly and to the rhythm of the music. This constant in-motion helps keep the dancer alert and in time to the music and thus better prepares him for what is to happen next.

4. The art of counterdancing, adjusting to the movement of the others in the square, is exceptionally important. In a pattern such as *around just one*, the inactives have the responsibility of adjusting to the movements of those who are active. They must move forward to get out of the way of those working behind them and they must move apart to allow a couple to move in between. They should move backward to permit the actives to work across within the center of the square.

5. If a dancer is taught in the early stages of learning to move to the beat of the music, his chance of becoming a good performer is greatly enhanced. The objective is not to see who can rush through a figure the fastest but rather to perform the figure smoothly, comfortably, and with a certain amount of grace.

6. It is a responsibility of the caller to set a tempo that allows for comfortable movements. It is also the responsibility of the caller to allow sufficient time for each movement to be done in a comfortable manner, and yet the calls should be timed in such a way that the dancers do not need to wait for the caller.

THE TEN COMMANDMENTS FOR SQUARE DANCERS

THOU SHALT — honor thy caller and harken to his voice, for thy success depends greatly upon his words.

THOU SHALT — exchange greetings and be friendly to all in thy group, lest ye be labeled a snob and unworthy of the title SQUARE DANCER.

THOU SHALT NOT — ridicule those dancers possessing two left hands but shall endeavor to help them distinguish one from the other.

THOU SHALT — strive to dance in different squares, thereby giving to all the benefit of thy fine personality and great experience.

THOU SHALT NOT — anticipate or dance ahead of thy caller for he is of fiendish nature and possessed of evil powers to make you appear ill-prepared in the eyes of thy fellow dancers.

THOU SHALT NOT — moan and belittle the caller, thy partner, nor the slippery floor when thou hast goofed, for this is likely thine own mistake.

THOU SHALT — clean thyself diligently before the dance, thereby creating a pleasant aroma for thy partner.

THOU SHALT — remain silent while thy caller gives advice and instructions.

THOU SHALT NOT — partake of strong drink before or during the dance, lest thy mind become befuddled and confused.

THOU SHALT — strive diligently to observe these commandments, and thy reward shall be great; for ye shall have many friends and shall be called SQUARE DANCER.

7. Learn Patter Calls

Most square dances today consist of two main parts, the figure and the breaks. The figure is usually repeated four times, and the breaks come at the beginning, midpoint and ending. For instance, the sequence of the dance would usually be as follows: (a) introduction, (b) figure, performed two times, (c) middle break, (d) figure, performed two times, and (e) ending. The introduction, middle break, and ending are usually very similar, if not identical.

With this information, the beginning caller can easily combine basic figures with introductions, breaks, and endings and call square dances of the desired difficulty. To assist the caller in doing this, some introductory, break, ending calls, and some figure calls are presented. The figure calls appear in order of difficulty. Some recommended patter records are listed at the end of the chapter.

INTRODUCTORY, BREAK, AND ENDING CALLS

1. All jump up and never come down,
   Swing your pretty girl 'round and 'round
   Allemande left with your left hand
   Right to your own, do a right and left grand
   Meet your own with a great big smile
   Promenade, go about a mile.

2. All join hands in a great big ring
   Circle 'round and 'round with the dear little thing
   Now do-si 'round the corner gal
   Then see-saw 'round your own little taw (*partner*)
   Do an allemande left with your left hand
   Then partner right for a right and left grand.

3. Left to the corner like swinging on a vine
   Swing the next gal down the line (*swing opposite gal*)
   Now a left to the next (*right-hand lady*) but pass her by
   Swing your own girl, swing her high.
   Allemande left with your left hand
   Partner right, right and left grand.

4. All join hands in a great big ring (*circle left*)
Circle 'round and 'round with the dear little thing
Now you're all goin' wrong on the wrong-way track
Go the other way back on the right-way track (*circle right*)
When you're home swing and whirl
Allemande with the corner maid
Meet your own and promenade.

5. Swing 'em four and swing 'em eight
Swing on the corner like swinging on a gate
Swing your own and promenade eight.

6. Eight hands up and 'round and 'round and 'round you go (*circle left*)
Now when you're home do a do-sa-do with the corner gal
Swing your own and here we go.

7. All join hands and circle to the south (*left*)
Let a little sunshine in your mouth
Half way 'round back track back
Single file, Indian style, with the lady in the lead (*left hand placed on left shoulder of person in front*)
When you're home, swing and whirl.

8. First you whistle, then you sing
All join hands and make a ring
Allemande left with your left hand
A right to your own for a right and left grand.

9. Big foot up, little foot down
Grab your own and swing 'em 'round
Right allemande that right-hand girl
Back to your own and give her a twirl
Left allemande and right-hand grand
And you promenade to beat the band.

10. Swing your honey 'round and 'round
Any old way but upside down, then
Promenade, go 'round and 'round.

11. Clap your hands (*twice*)
    Now slap your knees (*twice*)
    Bump-si-daisy if you please
    (*Partners bump hips together*)
    Swing on the corner high and low
    Swing your own, I told you so
    Now promenade.

12. Honor your partner, lady by your side
    All join hands and circle wide
    Spread right out like an old cow hide
    Break and trail along that line
    Lady in front and the gent behind
    Home you go you're doing fine
    You swing yours and I'll swing mine.

13. All eight balance, all eight swing
    Now promenade around the ring.

14. Swing your partner don't be late
    Swing on the corner like swingin' on a gate
    Now your own and promenade eight.

15. All join hands and circle to the south
    Let a little moonshine in your mouth
    Break and trail along that line
    When you get home what'll you do
    You swing her and she'll swing you.

16. Honor your partner, lady by your side
    All join hands and circle wide
    Break and trail along that line
    The lady in the lead and the gent behind
    Stop and swing when you get home
    Everybody swing your own.

Short Introductory Calls

1. Tighten up the belly bands loosen up the traces
   All join hands we're off to the races.

2. First you whistle, then you sing
Now all join hands and make a ring.

3. All jump up and never come down
Swing your honey, go 'round and 'round.

4. Up the river and around the bend
All join hands, we're gone again.

5. Lift your feet and set them down
Swing your honey, go 'round and 'round.

Short Ending Calls

1. Allemande left with your left hand
Bow to your partner and there you stand.

2. Stop where you are and don't be blue
The music quit, so I will too.

3. Honor your partner and your corner too
Now wave at the gal across from you
Thank you folks; I'm all through.

4. Promenade, you know where and I don't care
Take your honey to an easy chair.

5. Swing 'em hard and let 'em go
Take those gals to the old maids row.

6. That's all there is; the dance is ended
Go sit down 'cause the caller's winded.

7. Honor your partner, corners all
Honor your opposite across the hall
And that's it—that's all.

8. Promenade—you know where
And I don't care
Take her out and give her some air.

9. All you dancers listen to the call
   Thank you folks—that will be all.

FILL-IN PATTER

Command calls direct the dancers to perform specific movements. Fill-in patter is given between command calls and does not direct the dancers to perform movements. For example, in the following call the fill-in patter, sometimes referred to as a nonsense call, is shown in italics to set it off from the commands. "Allemande left with your left hand, then a right to your own for a right and left grand. *Hand over hand and heel over heel, the faster you go the better you feel.*" Following are fill-in patters to be used with the grand right and left, the promenade, and the swinging movements.

Right-and-Left-Grand Patter

These calls are used to fill in after the dancers have been directed to do a grand right and left.

1. Here we go on the heel and toe
   Hurry up, cowboys, don't be slow.

2. Right and left on the heel and toe
   Hi there Mary, Hello Joe.

3. Meet your Sally, meet your Sue
   Meet the little gal with the run-down shoe.

4. Hurry up, Grandpa, can't you see
   You're not as young as you used to be.

5. Big foot up and little foot down
   Make the big foot jar the ground.

6. Hand over hand and heel over heel
   The faster you go, the better you feel.

7. A right and left around the ring
   While the roosters crow and the birdies sing.

8. The right foot up and the left foot down
   Hurry up there or you'll never get around.

9. Hand over hand around the ring
   Meet your partner and everybody swing.

10. Here we go with the ol' red wagon
    Hind wheel broke and the axle draggin'.

Promenade Patter

1. Meet your honey and promenade eight
   Promenade eight 'til you get straight.

2. Meet that gal and promenade . . .
   Promenade that lady fair
   Promenade, go 'round the square.

3. Meet your gal and salute your Sue
   Now take that gal with the run-down shoe
   And promenade two by two.

4. Promenade, go two by two
   Now you walk 'em home like you used to do.

5. Meet your gal with a great big smile and promenade
   Promenade a mile, the gents run wild.

6. Meet your maid and promenade 'round
   Like a jay bird walking on frozen ground.

7. Meet your honey and don't be afraid . . .
   Take that gal and promenade.

8. Meet your gal and promenade—promenade
   Go 'round the ring, 'til the roosters crow and
   the birdies sing.

9. Meet your partner with a great big smile
Promenade boys go 'bout a mile.

10. Chicken on a fence and possum on a rail
Take your honey and away you sail.

11. Meet and swing and don't get cross
Promenade home with the guy who's boss.

12. Promenade, go 'round and 'round
Like a jay bird hoppin' on frozen ground.

13. She's that gal from ________ ____ City
Golly gee now ain't she pretty.

Swing Patter

1. Everybody swing and whirl
Swing 'round and 'round with your pretty little girl.

2. Swing 'em high and whirl 'em low
Keep on swinging your calico.

3. Swing your honey, go 'round and 'round
Lift her feet right off the ground.

4. Swing your gals with all your might
Swing 'em all day and swing 'em all night.

5. Swing 'em high and swing 'em low
Turn 'em loose and watch 'em go.

6. All jump up and never come down
Swing your pretty girl 'round and 'round.

7. Swing your gal, go 'round and 'round
Any old way but upside down.

Turn Back From a Right and Left Grand

1. Corn in a crib and wheat in a sack
   Meet your honey and turn right back.

2. With a hand in the hopper and a hand in the sack
   Meet your honey, go the other way back.

3. Meet your own with a hey, hey, hey
   Turn right back and go the other way.

SOME BASIC FIGURE CALLS

Around Two—Right and Left Thru

First and third go forward and back
Then forward again, pass thru, separate and go around two
Then same two forward again, right and left thru
Turn right around, do a right and left back
Same two ladies chain across
Same ladies chain back—identical track
Then allemande left with your left hand
Partners right for a right and left grand.

Around Two—Cross Trail

First and third go forward and back
Forward again, pass thru
Separate and go 'round two
Forward again, cross trail and you turn back
Forward again, cross trail, there's your corner
Left allemande, partners right for a right and left grand.

Texas Star

Ladies to the center, back to the bar
Gents to the center to a right-hand star
Now back to a left, but not too far
Wave to your own as you pass her by

Catch the next gal on the fly, in a star promenade
Now the gents back out and ladies swing in
Turn once and a half, then you're gone again (*ladies star left*)
Now the ladies back out, gents swing in
Turn once and a half and you're gone again
Gents step out and all four couples swing and whirl
Then allemande left with your left hand
Partners right for a right and left grand.
(Call four times to get original partners together.)

Half Sashay—Square Three-Quarters

Forward eight and back with you
Side couples go right and left thru
Sides rollaway
Half sashay
Heads go forward and back
Square three-quarters round
Separate, go 'round one
Stop behind the sides
Go forward and back
Two in the lead turn around
Allemande left

Half Square Thru—Frontier Whirl—Star Thru

Two and four go right and left thru
All four ladies chain
Two and four half square thru
Go right and left thru
Center four frontier whirl
Star thru
Go right and left through
Rollaway
Half sashay
Allemande left

Ladies Chain

First and third lead out to the right and circle four
You're doin' fine, head gents break and make a line
Forward eight and back with you
Forward again, do a right and left thru
Turn 'em 'round, do a right and left back, identical track
Two ladies chain across the square
Two ladies chain down the line
Two ladies chain across the set
Two ladies chain down the line
Then ladies to the center and back to the bar
Men to the center, right-hand star
Go all the way around, past your partner
Take the corner, allemande left with your left hand
Partners right for a right and left grand.

Wheel and Deal

Head two couples pass thru
Cross trail, go 'round just two
Make a line of four
Forward up and back you reel
Pass thru, wheel and deal
Just the girls, cross trail thru
To a left allemande
Partners right, right and left grand.

Substitute—Square Thru

Head ladies, you chain across
Side couples do a right and left thru
Heads to the right and circle to a line
Pass thru, then wheel and deal
Substitute . . .
Square thru, three-quarters 'round
Left allemande
Partners meet for a right and left grand.

Dive Thru—Pass Thru

First and third forward and back
Forward again, do a half square thru
Right and left thru with the outside two
Turn the girl, same two dive thru, pass thru
Then right and left thru with the outside two
Turn the girl, same two dive thru
Square thru, three quarters man
There's your corner, left allemande
Come back home for a right and left grand.

Star Thru—California Twirl

Promenade, go 'round the town
Listen now but don't slow down
Heads backtrack, sides wheel around
Promenade this pretty little girl
All backtrack and promenade the world
Heads backtrack, star thru, California twirl
With the girl you face box the gnat
Grand right and left right after that.

Catch All Eight

Join your hands and circle left
Circle left and hear me say
All four ladies half-sashay
Circle left in the same old way
Allemande left and don't be late
A right to your honey and catch all eight
A right-hand half, half-way 'round
Back by the left, go all the way 'round
A right to your corner and pull her by
And an allemande left with the one you met
Go right and left grand around the set.

Half Square Thru

From a promenade
One and three wheel around
Half square thru
Center two half square thru
Separate, go 'round one (face that two)
Half square thru
Bend the line, half square thru
Center two half square thru
Separate, go 'round one (face that two)
Square thru three-fourths 'round
Left allemande, right and left grand.

Multiple Movements

All four ladies chain
Head couples go to your right and circle forward
Head men break, make a line of four
Go forward eight and back
Pass thru and bend the line
Pass thru and bend the line again
Pass thru, wheel and deal
Double pass through
Cloverleaf
Double pass through
Centers in
Cast off three-quarters round
Star through
Double pass through
First go left, then the next go right
Go right and left through
Star through
Go right and left through
Swing through
Men trade
Turn through
Allemande left.

Multiple Movements

Four ladies chain through
Head couples star through
Go right and left through
Square three hands around
Split those two, go 'round one
Make a line of four
Go forward eight and back
Star through
Frontier whirl
Right and left through
Star through
Pass through
Bend the line
Go right and left through
Star through
Rollaway, half sashay
Star through
Frontier whirl
Go right and left through
Star through
Right and left through
Swing through
Spin the top
Right and left through
Slide through
Allemande left.

Multiple Movements

Head couples star through
Go right and left through
Pass through
Split those two, go 'round one
Make a line of four
Go forward eight and back
Box the gnat across from you
Right and left through
Square three hands round

Bend the line
Pass through
Wheel and deal
All eight make a U-turn back
Centers in
Cast off three-quarters 'round
Go forward and back
Star through
Frontier whirl
Double pass through
First go left and the next go right
Right and left through
Slide through
Allemande left.

Multiple Movements

Head couples pass through
Separate
Go 'round one
Make a line of four
Go forward eight and back
Star through
Pass through
Swing through
Girls trade and then men trade
Men run around that girl
Wheel and deal
Dive to the middle
Pass through
Go right and left through
Dive to the middle
Pass through
Do-sa-do all the way to an ocean wave
Spin the top
Spin the top again
Change hands
That's your corner
Allemande left.

Learn Patter Calls

Multiple Movements

Head couples go right and left through
Pass through
'Round two
Make a line of four
Go forward eight and back
Star through
Frontier whirl
Dive to the middle
Pass through
Go right and left through
Dive to the middle
Pass through
Swing through
Girls trade
Men trade
Men run around that girl
Wheel and deal
Dive to the middle
Pass through
Swing through
Swing through again
Change hands
That's your corner
Allemande left.

Multiple Movements

Head couples square through four hands 'round
Do-sa-do that corner girl all the way to an ocean wave
Spin change through and the girls circulate twice
Spin change through and the men circulate twice
Swing through
Girls circulate
Men trade
Swing through
Men circulate
Girls trade
Swing through

Girls circulate
Men trade
Turn through
Find your corner
Allemande left.

POPULAR PATTER RECORDS

Name	Record
"Possom Sop"	Grenn, 12045
"Railey Special"	Grenn, 12057
"New Mexico Hoedown"	Best, 104-A
"Crackerjack"	Blue Star, 1513-A
"One-Horse Reel"	Grenn, 12062
"Marldon"	TOP 25233
"Blllie John"	Wagon Wheel WW121
"Stay a Little Longer"	Kalox, k-1128-A
"Big Walker"	TOP, 25241
"Wildcat"	Windsor, 4186-A

8. Learn Singing Calls

This chapter contains a number of square dances that have been well established as popular dances. Some of them are considered old favorites in the sense that they have been popular for several years. Others have become popular only recently but are expected to remain popular for some time. The dances are arranged in approximate order of difficulty—a logical order for learning them.

OH JOHNNY MIXER

Record with calls: MacGregor, 652-A
Record without calls: Folkraft, 1037

Figure

All join hands and circle the ring (circle left) / Stop where you are and give your partner a swing / Swing that girl behind you (corner girl) / Then go home and you swing around your own / Do an allemande left with the corner girl / Then do-sa-do your own / All promenade with your sweet corner maid / Singing oh Johnny, oh Johnny, oh.

Sequence: Repeat the figure six times. (*This dance may be performed in either square or large-circle formation.*)

HOT TIME IN THE OLD TOWN TONIGHT

Record with calls: Windsor, 4415
Record without calls: Windsor, 4115

Opener

Let's all join hands and circle to the left / Break that ring and swing with the girl you love the best / Then you promenade back home with the cutest gal in sight / There'll be a hot time in the old town tonight.

Figure

Oh, the first couple right and circle four hands 'round / Pick up two more and circle six hands 'round / Pick up two more and circle eight hands 'round / There'll be a hot time in the old town tonight / It's the allemande left with the lady on your left (hey!) / Allemande right with the lady on your right (hey!) / Allemande left with the lady on your left (hey!) / Then a grand ol' right and left go 'round the ring / When you meet your honey, you do-sa-do around / Take her in your arms and swing her off the ground / Promenade back home with the sweetest gal in sight / There'll be a hot time in the old town tonight.

Closer

Now you all join hands, and stretch the ring w-a-y out / Rush in to the center—and everybody shout! / Back right out and swing, with the cutest gal in sight / There's been a hot time in the old town tonight! /

Sequence: Opener; repeat figure four times with first, second, third, and fourth couples leading, in that order; closer.

WABASH CANNONBALL

Record with calls: MacGregor, 007-2A
Record without calls: MacGregor, 614-A

Opener and Closer

Everybody swing your honey / You swing her high and low / Do an allemande with the old left hand / Around the ring you go / A grand old right and left, now listen to my call / You take your partner for a ride on the Wabash Cannonball (*promenade*).

Figure

First old couple out to the right, you circle for a while / On to the next, pick up two and watch those cowboys smile / On to the next, pick up two more and listen to my call / Now circle eight and don't be late on the Wabash Cannonball / All four couples separate, men back on the outside ring (*men reverse direction*) / When you meet your honey you give her a great big swing / Then do-sa 'round your corner, see-saw your partners all / Take your corner for a ride (*promenade*) on the Wabash Cannonball.

Sequence: Opener; figure repeated four times with first, second, third, and fourth couples leading in that order; closer.

JUST BECAUSE

Record with calls: Windsor, 4444
Record without calls: Windsor, 4144

Opener, Middle Break, and Closer

Walk all around your corner, she's the gal from Arkansas / See-saw 'round your partners, gents star right around that hall / And when you meet your corners, do a left allemande / Now walk around that circle with a right and left grand / When you meet your honey, do a do-sa-do / Step right up and swing her high and low / Then promenade that ring, throw your heads right back and sing (*all sing*) "Because, just because. . . ."

Figure

Well, the two head ladies chain right on over / Same two ladies chain back again / Side two ladies chain right on over / Same two ladies chain back again / Allemande left your corners, allemande right your partners / Go back and swing that sweet corner gal / Then promenade that corner, boys, shout and sing with joy (*all sing*) "Because, just because . . ." / (*tag, all sing*) "Because, just because. . . ." (*End figure with original corners for new partners.*)

Sequence: Opener, figure with head ladies, figure with side ladies, break, repeat figure with side ladies, repeat figure with head ladies; closer.

ALABAMA JUBILEE

Record with calls: Windsor, 4444
Record without calls: Windsor, 4144

Opener

Well, bow to your partner, the gal by your side / All join hands and circle left, you circle out wide / Walk all around that left-hand lady, see-saw 'round your taw / Back to the corner with your left hand, allemande left—go right and left grand / Right foot high, the left foot low, meet your honey and you do-sa-do / Do-sa-do on the heel and toe, then step right up and swing her, Joe / You swing her once, and swing her again, then promenade the ring / To the Alabama Jubilee, whoo-ee (*tag*) to the Alabama Jubilee.

Figure

Four little ladies promenade, go 'round the inside ring / Come back home and swing your man, you swing and you swing / Walk all around that left-hand lady, bow down to your own / Now swing your honey, go 'round and 'round, any ol' way but upside down / Four men promenade, you go 'round the inside ring / Come back home and do-sa-do, then corners you'll swing / Swing that corner 'round and 'round, then you promenade to town / To the Alabama Jubilee, oh, me (*tag*) to the Alabama Jubilee. (*Four ladies promenade ccw around inside of set back to partners; partners swing, walk all around corners, bow to partners, swing partners. Four gents promenade ccw around inside of set back to partners; partners do-sa-do; corners swing and promenade full around set back to gents' home positions, ending with all having original corners for new partners.*)

Middle Break and Closer

Well, turn the left-hand lady with the left-hand 'round, back to your honey with a right-hand 'round / Twice around your partners go, to the right-hand lady with a left elbow / Back to your honey and swing her, men, swing her quick, we're gone again / Allemande left with your left hand, here we go—right and left grand / Big foot high, little foot low, meet your gal and you do-sa-do / One time around on the heel and toe, then step right up and swing her, Joe / You swing her once, and swing her again, then promenade the ring / To the Alabama Jubilee, whoo-ee (*tag*) to the Alabama Jubilee.

Sequence: Opener; figure twice, break, figure twice; closer.

HURRY! HURRY! HURRY!

Record with calls: Windsor, 4405
Record without calls: Windsor, 4105

Opener

Everybody swing your corners, boys, swing 'em high and low / Swing the next girl down the line, don't let her go / Now go back home and swing your own, swing—and swing—and swing / Then promenade your pretty girl 'round the ring.

Figure

First old couple lead to the right, circle four hands 'round / Leave her there, go on to the next, circle three hands 'round / Take that couple on with you and circle five hands 'round / Now leave those four and join the line of three / The ladies chain across the hall, but don't return / Now chain again along that line just watch 'em churn / Now turn and chain across the hall, don't let 'em roam / Now chain the line and swing your honey home / Allemande left with the old left hand, and around that ring you go / It's a grand old right and left, boys, walk on the heel and toe / And when you meet that gal of yours, just do-sa-do / And then you promenade that pretty girl back home.

Sequence: Opener; repeat figure four times with first, second, third, and fourth couples leading in that order.

LITTLE SHOEMAKER

Record with calls: Windsor, 4441
Record without calls: Windsor, 4141

Opener, Break, and Closer

Swing . . . and swing, and swing, and promenade the ring / Dancing, dancing, all the day . . . / (*In*) The shoes that set your feet a-dancing, dancing . . . / Swing and dance your cares away. . . .

Figure

Whirl away, half sashay, circle left around that way / And you tap your feet (*tap, tap*) when you hear that beat (*tap, tap*) / See-saw 'round your new taw, do-sa-do your corners all / And you go back home, and swing your own . . . / Left allemande, step high—and pass your partner by / And swing and whirl, that next little girl / Left allemande, step high—and pass the last one by / And do-sa-do, with a brand new beau.

Sequence: Opener; figure, break, figure, break, figure, break, figure; closer.

GRAND-SQUARE QUADRILLE

Record with calls: Sets in Order, 102
Record without calls: Sets in Order, 102-B

Opener, Break, and Closer

Head couples right and left thru, across, and back / Side couples right and left thru, across, and back / Head couples to the right, right and left, thru and back / Side couples to the right, right and left, thru and back.

(*The grand-square movement—each line takes 16 counts.*)

(*Second Chorus*)
Head two ladies chain across and chain back / Side two ladies chain across and chain back / Head two ladies chain to the right and chain back / Side two ladies chain to the right and chain back.

(*Third Chorus*)
Two head couples half promenade, then right and left thru / Two side couples half promenade, then right and left thru / Two head couples half promenade, then right and left thru / Two side couples half promenade, then right and left thru.

Sequence: Grand square; first chorus; grand square; second chorus; grand square; third chorus; grand square.

OLD FASHIONED GIRL

Record with calls: Windsor, 4405-B
Record without calls: Windsor, 4015-B

Opener

Honor your old fashioned girl, hold her close, swing and whirl / Then promenade that ring / Now promenade single file, ladies in the lead and watch 'em smile / Gents step out, the ladies left-hand star / Do-sa-do your honey as she comes around to you / Swing her once or twice just like your Daddy used to do / Then you promenade that girl, she's just like the girl / That married dear old Dad.

Break and Closer

Do-sa-do your corner girl, go back home and swing and whirl / Swing the girl like dear old Daddy said / Allemande left with the ol' left hand / Partner right and a right and left grand / Hand over hand, around the ring you go / Now you do-sa-do the girl with the eyes so blue / Swing her 'round and 'round like your Daddy used to do / Then you promenade that girl, she's just like the girl / That married dear old Dad.

Figure

Head gents swing your maids, take those girls and promenade / Just half way 'round that ring / Right and left thru, right up the middle / Hurry up boys, keep time to the fiddle / Your left-hand ladies chain / All four ladies chain across the hall / Chain right back again, don't let 'em fall / Promenade this new little girl, she's just like the girl / That married dear old Dad.

Sequence: Opener, figure twice, break, figure twice, closer.

SOMEBODY ELSE'S DATE

Record with calls: Blue Star, 1557-A
Record without calls: Blue Star, 1557-B

Opener, Break, and Closer

Why don't you bow then swing with your partner, promenade single file / Girls back track around that world, gents step in behind your girl / Trail behind her . . . for awhile / Girls roll out, skip one man, corners all left, allemande / Grand right eight . . . go 'round the world / Then promenade with your sweetheart, for she's nobody else's girl.

Figure

First and third to the right and there you circle / Make a line, go forward up and back / Star right with the opposite pair, turn it once around out there / Back right out, circle eight around that track / The four gents will chain right on over, turn 'em left and corner promenade / I'd like to call you sweetheart but you're . . . somebody's else's date.

Sequence: Opener; figure twice with head couples, break, figure twice with side couples; closer.

IF YOU KNEW SUSIE

Record with calls: MacGregor, 911-A
Record without calls: MacGregor, 911-B

Opener, Break, and Closer

Join hands with Susie, circle left with Susie / Circle right, the other way 'round / Swing so classy with the gal with the gorgeous chassis / Allemande with the ol' left hand, partner right, a right and left grand / Meet Susie's sister and you meet her cousin Kate / Do-sa-do your own and allemande left, you don't be late / Come back and promenade with Susie / Go home with Susie / Oh, gee, what a gal.

Figure

Head couples bow to you two / Then right and left through / Let's turn 'em twice, sides right and left through / Four little ladies chain, three-quarters 'round the ring / Pull 'em right out, put 'em on the right / Circle eight, don't take all night / All around that corner girl / See-saw your pet / Allemande that corner, come back one and promenade / Promenade with Susie—go home with Susie / Oh, gee, what a gal.

Sequence: Opener; figure for heads, figure for sides, break, figure for sides, figure for heads; closer.

IF IT FEELS GOOD DO IT

Record with calls: Dance Ranch, 609-A
Record without calls: Dance Ranch, 609-B

Opener

Walk all around your corner, turn your partner by the left / Four ladies chain about three-quarters 'round / Now when you turn that lady there, four ladies chain across / Turn the gal around right there, and sides face grand square / If it feels good, left allemande / Swing and promenade tonight / There's really no mystery to it / Square dancing's just a better way of life.

Figure

Those heads promenade go half way / Rollaway and now slide through / Go right and left thru, turn and rollaway / Curlique and make a star, go full around you, do / And if it feels good, girls turn back and swing / Swing and promenade tonight / There's really no mystery to it / Square Dancing's just a better way of life.

Sequence: Opener; figure twice, break, figure twice; closer.

DON'T LET THE GOOD LIFE PASS YOU BY

Record with calls: Dance Ranch, 601-A
Record without calls: Dance Ranch, 601-B

Opener, Middle Break, and Closer

(*Sides face grand square*)
Did you ever lie and listen to the rainbow / Did you ever eat a homemade apple pie / Did you ever hold a child while he was sleeping / Just don't let the good life pass you by (*allemande*) / Left allemande and weave around that ring, go / Do a do-sa-do and promenade you fly / Did you ever take the time to help a neighbor / Just don't let the good life pass you by.

Figure

And now those heads square thru, count four hands in the middle you do / And with the sides swing thru, I say / Boys run, bend the line, go up and back in time / Slide thru then a right and left thru that way / Ladies lead do a flutter wheel, go full around and swing your corner / Promenade / Did you ever squeeze her hand while you were dancing / Just don't let the good life pass you by.

Sequence: Opener; figure twice, break, figure twice; closer.

CHIME BELLS

Record with calls: TOP, 25174-A
Record without calls: TOP, 25174-B

Opener, Break, and Closer

Walk around that corner, then you see-saw your taw / Join hands circle 'round that hall / Allemande the corner, do-sa-do your own / Four men star by the left around you go / Turn the partner by the right and go left allemande / Come back and promenade around the ring (all the way) / Chime bells are ringing on the mountain so high / Upon a summer's eve.

Figure

Four ladies chain, turn a little girl and then / Heads promenade half way you go / Down the middle go right and left thru, turn the gal I say / Star thru, pass thru, circle up four half way / Swing that corner girl and go left allemande / Come back do-sa-do and promenade / Chime bells are ringing, on the mountain so high / Upon a summer's eve.

Alternate ending: Sleep my little lady on a mountain so high / Upon a summer's eve.

Sequence: Opener; figure twice, break, figure twice; closer.

TEXAS PLAINS

Record with calls: Windsor, 4891-A
Record without calls: Windsor, 4891-B

Opener, Break and Closer

Your corner do-sa-do and then you see-saw your own / The men star right one time / Now turn your partner by the left, your corner by the right / Your partner left an allemande thar / Men back up in a right hand star / You back the star 'round the land, slip the clutch left allemande / Come home do-sa-do and promenade / Promenade home out where the buffalo roam / Out on the Texas plains.

Figure

Heads (sides) square thru, four hands around you do / To the outside two swing thru / Rock it, don't be late, boys trade, girls circulate / Turn thru and go left allemande / Come back home and do-sa-do, it's once around you go / Swing the corner girl and promenade / You'll take her back home out where the buffalo roam / Out on the Texas plains.

Sequence: Opener; figure twice for heads, break, figure twice for sides; closer.

STREET FAIR

Record with calls: Jay-Bar-Kay, 139-A
Record without calls: Jay-Bar-Kay, 139-B

Opener, Middle Break, Closer

Join hands circle, you circle around that ring / Allemande left your corner, come home a do-sa-do / Men star by the right hand, go once around and then / Left allemande, you weave around the town / Join the crowd you see / Do-sa-do, promenade for me / Can't you hear the sound of the merry-go-round / Well, join us at the fair.

Figure

Now one and three (two and four) lead to the right and circle to a line / Forward eight, come on back, star thru in time / Do-sa-do, go once around and then swing thru / Boys trade, boys run, bend the line you see / Slide thru, pass thru, the corner lady swing / Left allemande, come on back and promenade / Can't you hear the sound of the merry-go-round / Well, join us at the fair.

Sequence: Opener; figure twice, break, figure twice; closer.

POPULAR SINGING CALL RECORDS

Name	Record	Caller
"Street Fair"	Jay Bar Kay # 139	Kent Anderson
"Texas Plains"	Windsor # 4891	Bob Van Antwerp
"Chime Bells"	TOP # 25174	Reath Blickenderfor
"Don't Let the Good Life Pass You By"	Dance Ranch # 601	Frank Lane
"Somebody Else's Date"	Blue Star # 1557	Marshall Flippo
"Old Black Magic"	Hi Hat # 339	Bill Peterson
"The Best Things in Life Are Free"	MacGregor # 2055	Jim Mayo
"Gentle on My Mind"	Wagon Wheel # 113	Don Franklin
"Summer Sounds"	MacGregor # 2051	Bob Dawson
"Wheels"	Old Timer # 8167	Johnny Schultz
"Love in the Country"	Wagon Wheel # 303	Beryl Main
"If It Feels Good Do It"	Dance Ranch # 609	Frank Lane

9. Improve Techniques of Calling

As the caller you become the leader of the dancers, thus acquiring the responsibility of helping them not only to enjoy dancing but also to dance well. Calling has certain prerequisites that every prospective caller should meet before moving into this interesting activity:

1. Be an experienced dancer. If you are to teach square dancing, you must not only understand it but be able to analyze the patterns and know the terminology to explain them clearly. Your directions must be clear, concise, and easy to follow.

2. Be excited, enthusiastic, and dedicated to square dancing. Your enthusiasm in calling and teaching will often determine whether the dancers remain interested in the activity.

3. Be a leader. A few characteristics of leadership that should be emphasized are courtesy, sense of humor, patience with those who do not understand the call the first time, ability to encourage when necessary, and ability to sense how fast the group can progress.

4. Don't be afraid of hard work. It takes effort to master the technicalities of wording, phrasing, timing, dance movements, rhythm, and tone.

The question is often asked how long one should dance before attempting to teach and call. At least a year of dancing is recommended. Two years are better, but this is an individual matter, depending on how often you dance and how dedicated a student you are of square dance. It is an injustice to the dancers to impose inferior calling upon them because of your insufficient experience.

You should ask yourself the following challenging questions: Am I ready to call and teach? Do I like people and want to help them enjoy recreational activity under my direction? Am I willing to work hard to learn the fundamentals of square dancing movements so that I can call easily and rhythmically?

If you answer these questions in the affirmative, you are on the threshold of a very interesting and rewarding experience.

KINDS OF CALLS

The kinds of calling currently in use are these: (1) prompting calls, (2) singing calls, and (3) patter calls (harmonic chant or talking call).

The *prompting call* is the oldest kind of call and is best known in the New England States where it is used in contra work. The prompter calls only the name of each movement just before the dancers perform it. In square dancing the grand square movement is done to the prompting call, "Grand square!" The dancers start the movement on the first count of the next phrase. Sixteen counts are required to complete the movement.

The *singing call* is a song with the lyrics replaced by square-dance directions. The caller sings the directions to the melody of the song. Some callers use less melody and more of a harmonic chant with the singing call because this affords additional freedom to stylize the calls.

The *patter call* has no fixed pattern that restricts the caller. The caller talks or chants in time to the music, and gives whatever square dance directions he chooses. He emphasizes the *directional (command) calls* and fills in with *nondirectional calls*, known as fill-in patter. Following is an example:

> Allemande left with your left hand (command)
> Here we go in a right and left grand (command)
> Right and left on the heel and toe (filler)
> Hurry up cowboys, don't be slow (filler)
> Meet your maid and you promenade 'round (command)
> Like a jay bird walking on frozen ground (filler)

The harmonic chant is the most commonly used patter-call technique, requiring a rhythmical chant and musical, dominant-tone voice pitch. These are easily executed with the weak melody and the strong beat of patter-call music.

Improve Techniques of Calling

Learning to Call

What are some of the basic requirements of the beginning caller?

1. You must learn to enunciate clearly so that the dancers can understand the command. A common problem with beginning callers is failure to isolate the command words from the non command words so that the commands stand out clearly for the dancers to follow. "ALLEMANDE LEFT with your left hand—Here we go in a RIGHT AND LEFT GRAND." The key words are accented.

2. You must be aware of the BEAT at all times. Play a square dance record that has a clear, strong beat and clap in rhythm to the music. Also tap your heel in time with the music; this is a technique most callers use. Listen for the accumulative phrasing of 4, 8, 16, 32 and 64.

3. Select easy calls and start calling them to music. Write out your call and underline the syllable falling on the accent. "Swing your partner round and round." Say the command in rhythm to the music. The downbeat is on count one and the upbeat on count two. Give your imaginary dancers correct amounts of time to get through the formations.

4. Put away your call sheet when you actually call for dancers. Reading a call from a call sheet in public is unacceptable because the caller must keep his eyes on the dancers to gauge his own timing and to make sure the dancers are following the calls.

5. Using a tape recorder as you practice your calls is invaluable. Play back your calls and listen to the tone and rhythm. You will learn what your best friends may hesitate to tell you. After you are more experienced, tape several calls and join with a group of your friends in dancing to these calls. You will quickly find whether you are ready to take the next step—live calling.

TECHNICAL ASPECTS OF CALLING

Let's approach the technical aspects of square dance calling from three points of view: (1) the principles underlying calling technique, (2) the performance of the caller in actual practice, and (3) the matter of policy in the use of material and in dance and group procedures.

Principles

Technical principles underlie three areas of square dance calling: time, tone, and temper (mood and style).

Time (rhythm). Rhythm exists in many aspects of life, including day and night, ebb and flow of the tide, the changing seasons, a person's walking gait, and his pattern of speech. Rhythm is fundamental to square-dance calling.

Tempo. In selecting records, adjusting the phonograph turntable, or instructing the orchestra, the caller will determine the speed of his call (and the dance). His judgment will be influenced by: the dance (figure)—its form and mood; the dancers—their experience, condition, and mood; the region—its prevailing practices.

To determine the tempo of a record, count the beats for thirty seconds by your watch and multiply by two. To check the accuracy of your turntable, use a "strobo" disc, or attach a bit of adhesive tape to the edge and check the revolutions per minute by your watch: 78, 45, 33 1/3.

Rhythm. Rhythm is basically an inherited characteristic; however, evidence exists that it can be cultivated to some extent. But no person lacking a basic sense of rhythm should aspire to square-dance calling.

The guide to the caller's rhythm is the music. It is imperative that he hear the beat and that he be aware of it almost unconsciously so that he can give attention to the more variable aspects of his work. While being "on the beat" is fundamental, the experienced caller will get artistic effects by violating the basic rhythm in subtle ways—syncopation, delay, and double time as examples.

Phrasing. The music to which we dance is phrased, with groups of beats constituting a measure, groups of measures forming a longer phrase, verses and choruses still longer phrases. Most phrases are built on the scale of 4, 16, 32, 64.

The caller of square dance is largely concerned with the four-beat phrase. His problem is to recognize the beat and make his call coincide with it.

The basic phrase in music is indicated by the musical signature:

two-four (two beats to a measure; a quarter note receives one count), *three-four* (three beats to a measure; a quarter note receives one count), *four-four* (four beats to a measure; a quarter note receives one count), *six-eight* (six beats to a measure; an eighth note receives one count), and so forth.

Three-four time is useful to the caller only for the waltz quadrilles (which have far more to offer than their current limited use indicates). But even here, as in all others listed above, the caller is interested in the *four-beat* phrase. Thus he takes two measures in two-four time, four in three-four, one in four-four, and two in six-eight to complete his phrase of patter.

The four-beat phrase is significant (and can be recognized) because none of its beats receive the same stress. In order of emphasis they are 1, 3, 2, 4. Therefore, the first stressed word of the caller's phrase of patter should fall on the first beat of the measure of music in four-four time, or the first beat of a two-measure group in two-four or six-eight time. Since count 3 is second in emphasis, the caller may use it to begin his phrase without too much discomfort, but if he begins on either of counts 2 or 4, he fights the music and makes trouble both for himself and the dancers.

Timing. Timing is the matter of executing the call so that dancers have directions for their actions early enough to lead them but not so early as to rush or lose them. The caller will need to: (1) watch the dancers carefully, (2) harmonize the timing with an "average" performance of the crowd, (3) dispose of conflicts between timing and phrasing, and (4) develop his ability for split-second judgment.

Tone. Just as rhythm is produced by the regular recurrence of beats, so is musical tone; the only difference is that the latter is vastly more rapid. While the harmonic or tonal chant involves tone in more varied ways, all kinds of calling are concerned with tone.

Support. The human body is a musical instrument, providing a resonance and richness of overtone which the vocal chords alone cannot produce. There are techniques of voice use which the caller ought to cultivate. A teacher of vocal music or public speaking could offer some very helpful suggestions.

Relaxation is important, for tension tends to make the voice thin and high pitched. Deep breathing and regulation of the air column by diaphragm control will help to give the voice the support it needs.

Fortunately the science of electronics has provided another means of voice support. With amplification the caller can (and should) use a lighter, more pleasant, more flexible and deeper tone than was ever possible to the old-time callers. Converting the microphone from an enemy to a friend is sometimes a long and arduous task, but the results can be very beneficial.

Quality. The importance of a pleasant, well-modulated, exciting voice cannot be overemphasized. Even the person who inherits either a light, thin voice or a harsh voice can apply disciplines which will produce a manageable and effective calling style, especially since the microphone is available.

Clarity. Enunciation is very important. Persons unaccustomed to public speaking have particular trouble remembering to exaggerate lip and tongue movements to produce sounds legible to a large group. A little enunciation practice of the kind used by radio announcers is helpful. In this connection we should emphasize that naturalness is a distinct asset. Artificial-sounding pronunciations are neither becoming nor convincing.

There is the additional problem, previously discussed, of isolating the *command* words from the rest of the patter, so that they stand out sharply to direct the dancers' actions.

Pitch. Pitch is to music what tempo is to rhythm: the rate or frequency of the beats. The pitch of middle C on the piano is produced by a vibration of 261 beats per second.

The caller will want to determine his own comfortable voice range, select his music, and govern his style accordingly. The *prompting* and *conversational* callers need only to keep the voice in a pleasant and effective range. The *singing* caller will find his record sources limited to some degree by his ability to sing melody. The caller who uses the *harmonic chant* will need to select music to which he can pitch effectively. Harmonics are most effective in combination with conversational chanting.

The skillful caller will achieve artistic effects by the subtle violation of the rules of harmony. Mild dissonances, quickly resolved, produce a pleasurable and exciting effect.

Temper. Probably the secret of the expert caller lies in the intangibles of mood and personality. Analyzed, however, many of the qualities related to these intangibles can be purposely produced.

Variety. In the choice of materials, in the use of patter, and in the handling of the voice, use variety. It is achieved by preparation for each assignment, by drill in new effects, and by guarding against ruts in one's performance.

Excitement. Excitement is not necessarily achieved by "pouring it on" with furious intensity. It is much more likely to result from the sincere enthusiasm of the caller who loves the dance and wants the dancers to have fun and especially from the use of the many little tricks of time and pitch used by the experts.

Participation. The caller, like the public speaker, must "get across" to his audience. Communication results from the ability of the caller to enter into the mood of the dancers, sharing in their fun and being one of them. He submerges his own personality in the interest of the dance. The prima donna is totally out of place as a caller.

Style. While you can learn much from observing the experts and listening to their records, the caller ought not to become merely an imitator. You will be your best by being yourself. You need to follow good procedures and sound advice while cultivating your own potential strengths as a caller.

Performance

The first drill for the caller is dancing. You need a rich background of experience on the floor to do a good job at the microphone. Then you need to find the time, and a place to call, both privately and (when you are ready) publicly. But remember, a premature passion for the caller's fee could be your undoing.

While you can improve your calling by working at it while driving a car, you ought to do most of your practice with the record player and microphone. A tape recorder provides an excellent check on performance, exposing faults ruthlessly.

In terms of personality, we suggest only that you possess and demonstrate the fine qualities which one respects in a group leader. He is the epitome of humility, patience and courtesy. Furthermore, he is (or is expected to be) skilled in his particular activity; he is a congenial host, a master of ceremonies, and a disciplinarian.

Policy

In the selection of materials the caller will need to be alert to trends in the square dance, and he will need to know where to stop in the tendency toward the elaboration and proliferation of dances and dance movements.

The caller structures the program out of miscellaneous component parts. Each part should flow smoothly into the next. The dance program should be balanced in variety, and it should end while the dancers are wishing for more. It ought to have many elements of fun in it, and it ought to be built with imagination and with special touches of interest and surprise to delight the crowd.

In terms of personal and social values, square dancers are generally fun-loving, wholesome people. To foster this kind of atmosphere, the caller's policy should be to avoid the following situations: (1) compromise with unwholesome associations, (2) too much competition, and (3) commercialism which places the economic motive above other considerations.

Never in history have people so desperately needed the friendly human relationships which square dancing offers. Its future is largely in the caller's hands.

10. Improve Techniques of Teaching

The perpetuation of square dancing is directly dependent upon those who teach it. The teacher not only helps people to learn the particular skills of square dancing, but he also has considerable influence on the development and retention of interest in the activity. Expert teaching is vital to the growth of square dancing as an educational and recreational pursuit.

RULES OF GOOD TEACHING

1. Be enthusiastic, and try to spread your enthusiasm to the dancers.

2. Have the content well prepared so that the dancers do not become discouraged because of your lack of preparation and organization.

3. Pay adequate attention to the physical arrangements, especially the phonograph and speaking system.

4. Remember, square dancers want to dance; they do not want to listen to lectures or spend too much time doing drills. Insofar as possible, let them learn while they dance.

5. Be sure to teach material which is neither too easy nor too difficult for the particular dancers; otherwise, they will become either disinterested or discouraged.

6. Remember you have two basic responsibilities: to teach people to dance and to keep them interested and motivated.

TEACHING BEGINNING MOVEMENTS

People learn best by doing; therefore, the dancers should become active as quickly as possible. In a one-hour session beginning dancers can learn several basics and enjoy dancing them. A good procedure is to form all of the dancers into one large circle facing toward the center and alternating men and women. This gets everybody involved and the teacher-caller need be concerned with only one formation and one group. By demonstrating and then using the microphone, you can talk the dancers through the following calls, first without music, then with music: honor your partner, honor your corner, do-sa-do your partner, do-sa-do your corner, swing your partner, swing your corner, circle left, circle right, promenade single file, and couples promenade. Following these movements, have every second couple do an about face and have the couples facing each other circle up four. From these small circles you can teach the ladies chain, right and left through, right hand star, left hand star, and pass through. Now you are ready to have each circle of four pick up four more and circle eight. Then square the sets and review the same movements in the formation.

Following is an example of calls that might be used to lead the dancers through some elementary movements after the squares have been formed:

Honor your partner — —
Lady by your side — —
Join your hands and circle wide
— — — —

All the way 'round the ring you go
On the heel and on the toe
When you're home you swing and whirl
Go 'round and 'round with the pretty little girl.

One and three go forward and back
Make those feet go what-a-dee-whack
Two and four go forward and back
— — — —.

One and three two ladies chain
Turn 'em around and here we go
Chain 'em back on a heel and toe
— — — —.
(*Repeat for side ladies*)

Now left allemande with your left hand
Here we go in a right and left grand
Right and left go 'round the ring
'Til the roosters crow and the birdies sing.

Then promenade, go two by two
Take that girl along with you
When you're home you swing and whirl
Go 'round and 'round with the pretty little girl.

Now do-sa-do your corners all
See-saw your pretty little taw
Swing on the corner like swinging on a gate
And now your own if you're not too late.

First and third forward and back
— — — —
Then forward again do a right and left thru
— — — —.

(Repeat with couples 2 and 4.)
(Repeat with couples 1 and 3.)
Repeat with couples 2 and 4.)

By this time the dancers will be ready to learn some of the patter call figures in chapter 7 (the figures are approximately in the order of difficulty) and some of the elementary singing calls in chapter 8.

At this point you, as the teacher, ought to refer back to the fundamentals in chapter 3 and to the fifty basics in chapter 4 and decide which movements to teach next. The fifty basics are listed approximately in the order they should be taught; however, considerable room exists for individual preference in this matter.

As dancers learn additional movements, remember that they enjoy doing the things they already know in addition to learning some new movements. You should be very sensitive to the correct balance of teaching new material and having fun with the material that has already been learned. Keep the dancers challenged but at the same time help them enjoy themselves by dancing the movements they know.

TEACHING MORE ADVANCED MOVEMENTS

Experienced dancers usually learn new movements quickly because they have become "dance oriented" and they have a wealth of experience on which to build new knowledge. This situation presents an additional challenge to you as the teacher. One of the pitfalls in connection with experienced dancers is the idea that they will never lose interest. But it is a fact that many once-motivated dancers have become discouraged and disinterested because of a poor job done by their teacher-caller.

Anybody, regardless of how experienced he is, must continue to be challenged if he is to retain interest in an activity. In this situation, you must be extremely sensitive to the desires of the group, realizing that to some extent you can mold their tastes and interests, but at the same time you must take careful direction from their responses. Specifically you should do the following: (1) Watch for facial expressions that tell you about the dancer's responses; (2) Watch the style with which they go through the movements and determine whether they are enthusiastic and excited or whether they are just going through the motions; (3) Listen carefully to conversations with the dancers and be very sensitive to their suggestions. Even try to read between the lines of their comments to determine the extent to which they are satisfied with your teaching.

THE ONE-NIGHT STAND (SQUARE DANCE PARTY)

Conducting a one-night stand or a square-dance party for a group is in many ways more difficult than conducting a regular club meeting for an advanced group. Those participating in a one-night stand are usually inexperienced dancers, and many of them know virtually nothing about the activity. Yet these people are there to have a good time, and they expect the leader to provide it for them. The following are some guidelines that will help make "one-nighters" a success:

1. Keep explanations and drills to a minimum. Give just enough directions to teach the movements well enough for the dancers to do them.

2. Do not strive for perfection. Concentrate on helping the participants have a good time in the hope that they will develop interest in the activity.

3. Keep everyone actively involved. There should be no watchers and no idle would-be participants.

4. Keep the dances simple in order that the participants will not become discouraged or embarrassed about their inability to perform the movements.

5. Be outgoing but not overbearing, in order to establish a feeling of oneness between you and the participants.

6. Progress from the very simple movements to the more complex ones, as far as possible within the time limitation. This will help give the dancers a feeling of accomplishment as well as a good time.

7. For the most interesting kind of program, alternate round dances with square dances.

8. Have planned procedures to allow the participants to change partners in an orderly manner, but do not have them change partners or positions too often; this will contribute to their confusion.

The sample patter calls stated earlier in this chapter could be used to good advantage in a one-night stand. In addition, many of the easier calls in the basic fifty described in chapter 4 could be used. Some of the easier singing calls presented in Chapter 8 could also be used. And some dances from the list of standard round dances near the end of this chapter should be used to alternate with the square dances.

ROUND DANCING

For a long time, round dances have been an important part of square dancing. Some people view round dancing as an activity to simply add variety to a two-to-three-hour square dance session. But for most dancers this is not the case, for round dancing is an interesting activity by itself—one that requires a set of skills unique to this particular form of dance. Many people enjoy round dancing as much as square dancing. Both forms of dance are more appealing when they are alternated with each other.

Typically then, a square dance session would consist of mostly square dancing, but with the square-dance tips broken up periodically by a round dance. Ordinarily four to six round dances will be included in an evening of square dancing.

Several old favorite round dances should be familiar to all square dancers. Some of them are listed below.

Title	Record Company and Number
Mexican Hat Dance	Cameo 149B
Jiffie Mixer	Windsor 4684
Tennessee Wig Walk	Decca 28846
Teton Stomp	Windsor 4615
Left Footers One Step	Windsor 4650
I Miss My Swiss	Coral 9-605-40
Dancing in the Street	RCA 47-7474
Miss Frenchie Brown	A & M 870

In addition to these old favorites, new round dances are being prepared constantly to popular tunes. Some of these have great appeal and are very popular for a period of time. One of these current dances is selected each month by Sets In Order (The American Square Dance Society) as the Round of the Month. Many teachers throughout the nation teach the Round of the Month on a regular basis.

It is vital for the teacher to remember that round dancing is not simply a time filler, and neither is it simply a break from square dancing. Round dancing is important in itself; some people even prefer it to square dancing. A wise and dedicated square-dance teacher will give appropriate attention to round dances as an important part of a square-dance program.

11. Conduct Exhibition Square Dancing

Conduct Exhibition Square Dancing

Lloyd Shaw brought an element of showmanship to square dancing with the choreography he used for the Cheyenne Mountain Dancers. He set the stage for other groups to participate in exhibition square dancing.

Possibly the Brigham Young University dancers have done more than any others to carry exhibition square dances throughout the United States and Europe, having completed numerous tours within this country and nine performance tours to Europe.

Exhibition square dancing is the performance of specially choreographed dances which are made up primarily of standard square-dance movements but which have lifts, flourishes, and other colorful aspects added in order to make the dances highly entertaining and challenging. This style of square dance can serve two important purposes: (1) It is interesting and challenging to those who choreograph and perform it. (2) It is an enjoyable form of entertainment for those who appreciate such performances.

The calls for an exhibition square dance are not "hot hash" but rather they are a combination of basics put together in tight sequence with extras added to make the calls interesting and entertaining. The calls are written in such a way that every beat of each measure is accounted for. Even though the calls are done to patter music, the caller must know them so thoroughly that he calls with consistent timing and rhythm every time. After the caller and the dancers have all learned their parts reasonably well, some flexibility relative to timing can be applied by the caller.

A call sheet is permissible for this kind of work until the caller has memorized the calls and the timing. After the dance has been learned in proper sequence and exact timing, the caller can use syncopation, change terminology, or make other adjustments so long as the counts and movements remain the same.

Other important points of information are these: (1) On a small stage, only one square will fit because of the amount of space needed for some of the lifts. (2) Be sure not to regiment the dancers and formalize the calls to such a point that the dance seems like a drill.

Following are the instructions and calls for one exhibition square dance which has been very popular and has been used extensively to entertain audiences throughout the United States and in countries of Europe. Calls and descriptions of other choreographed exhibition square dances may be obtained from the authors upon request. Unfortunately, lack of space does not permit the inclusion of other dances in this book. A creative dance teacher can utilize information from this chapter to assist him in choreographing exhibition square dances for his own particular purposes.

CALL SHEET IN BRIEF

NAME: MERRY BEE
NATIONALITY: American
CHOREOGRAPHED BY: Mary Bee Jensen

4 Count Introduction

Honor your partner — —
Lady by your side — —
One and three you bow and swing
Go round and round with the dear
little thing.

Go down the center swap and swing
— — — —
Face the sides, split those two
Around one stand four in line.

Sashay into the middle of the set
Sashay back, you're not thru yet
Sashay in and you form a row

The girls reach back and there's
your beau.

Heel and toe and out you go
Heel and toe and in you go
Heel and toe and out you go
Heel and toe and in you go.

Sashay back to places all
Pass right thru across the hall
Right and left back on a heel and toe
Turn 'em around and don't be slow.

Chain the ladies down the line
Turn 'em around, you're doing fine
Chain them back on a heel and toe
Chain them back and here we go.

Ladies chain across the set
Turn them boys, you're not thru yet
Chain them back on a heel and toe
Turn them around and get ready Joe.

Ladies to the center and form a ring
Circle right like everything
Men to the left, pass her by
Stoop down low and left her high.

Girls fan out like a great big rose
Hold it there and take a pose
Hold on tight and let her down
Till her feet will touch the ground.

Allemande L, the ladies star
Gents run around but not too far
Allemande L, the four gents star
Ladies run around but not too far.

Allemande L with your L hand
Here we go in a R and L grand

R and L go round the ring
Till you meet your maid and promenade.

Join your hands and circle R
Men step in make a circle there
Pick up your girl in the air
Circle round — — .

— — — —
— — — —
— — — —
— — (down on 15 & 16).

Now promenade but don't slow down
Promenade, go 2 by 2
Men reach in form a L hand star
Pick up your girl right where you are.

(16 counts—Kings cross)

— — — —
— — — —
— — — —
— — — —

Now put her down and swing at home
Everybody swing your own
Swing her high, swing her low
Swing your gal in Calico.

One and three star by the right
Pick up your corner with an arm around
Star promenade go round the town
— — — — .

Outside gent roll back one
Come on boys let's have some fun
Lonesome lady roll back one
Keep on going fun fun fun.

Reverse that line reverse that star
You're going wrong the way you are
— — — —
— — — — .

Reverse that star reverse, that line
Hold on tight, you're doin' fine
— — — —
Jessie Polka here we go.

With a heel and a toe you can
Start the room a jumpin' —
When those ladies swing right back
You can hear their bustles bumpin' —.

With a heel and a toe
Your heart is really in it
When you start to swing it—
To the Jessie Polka Dance.

Men back out and form a line
Circle forward, circle back
Ladies bow, gents know how
Pick 'em up and swing and whirl.

— — — —
— — — —
— — — —
— — — — .

Now put her down and circle back
One big circle that's what you do
When you're home you swing and whirl
Go round and round with the pretty girl.

— — — —
— — — —
— — (Whirl out 11-12)
Sit 13-14, pose 15-16.

MERRY BEE—EXHIBITION SQUARE

Music: "Chicken Plucker" Record # 734

To begin the dance, the starting positions are W to R of M. Whenever hands are free, M should place his on back pockets with palms out. W should hold skirt out wide, waist high. Begin on L ft for both M and W. Most of the dance is either a polka-in-place step for each count or a walk step. The first portion of the dance will be done in polka steps as the couples move. Those not progressing will do the polka-in-place *until they start the lifts.* Thereafter, the couples maintain a walk step. (See description on lifts and special terms at end of dance before beginning to teach dance.)

Fig	Cts	Call	Description
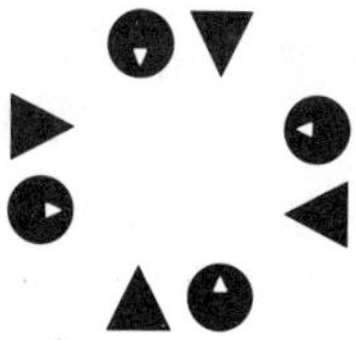 1	4	Honor your partner	Bow to your partner. M hold W's L hand.
	4	Lady by your side	Bow to your corner W (corner W is on M's L side), keeping hold of partner's hand.
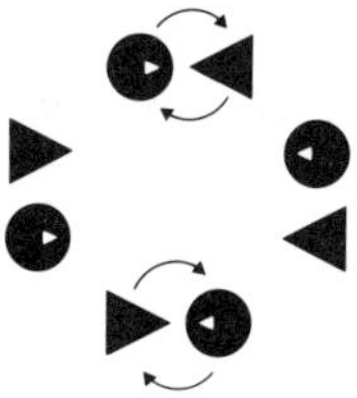 2a	8	And now it's head couples swing a little while Hey! Say you make 'em smile	Couples 1 & 3 swing partner in home position full 8 cts in R swing. Couples 2 & 4 do polka-in-place for 24 cts. (See description page)
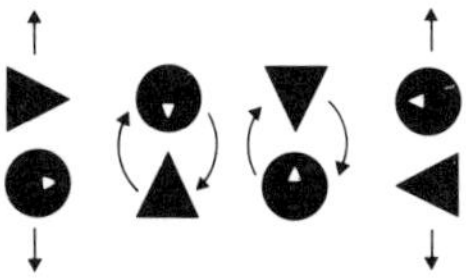 2b	16	Go down the center swap and swing — — — — Face the sides, split those two Around one stand four in line	(1 & 3 swap and swing 8 cts.) Couples 1 & 3 polka toward each other. Begin on L, polka 4 cts. M 1 swings W 3; M 3 swings W 1; swing 4 cts.

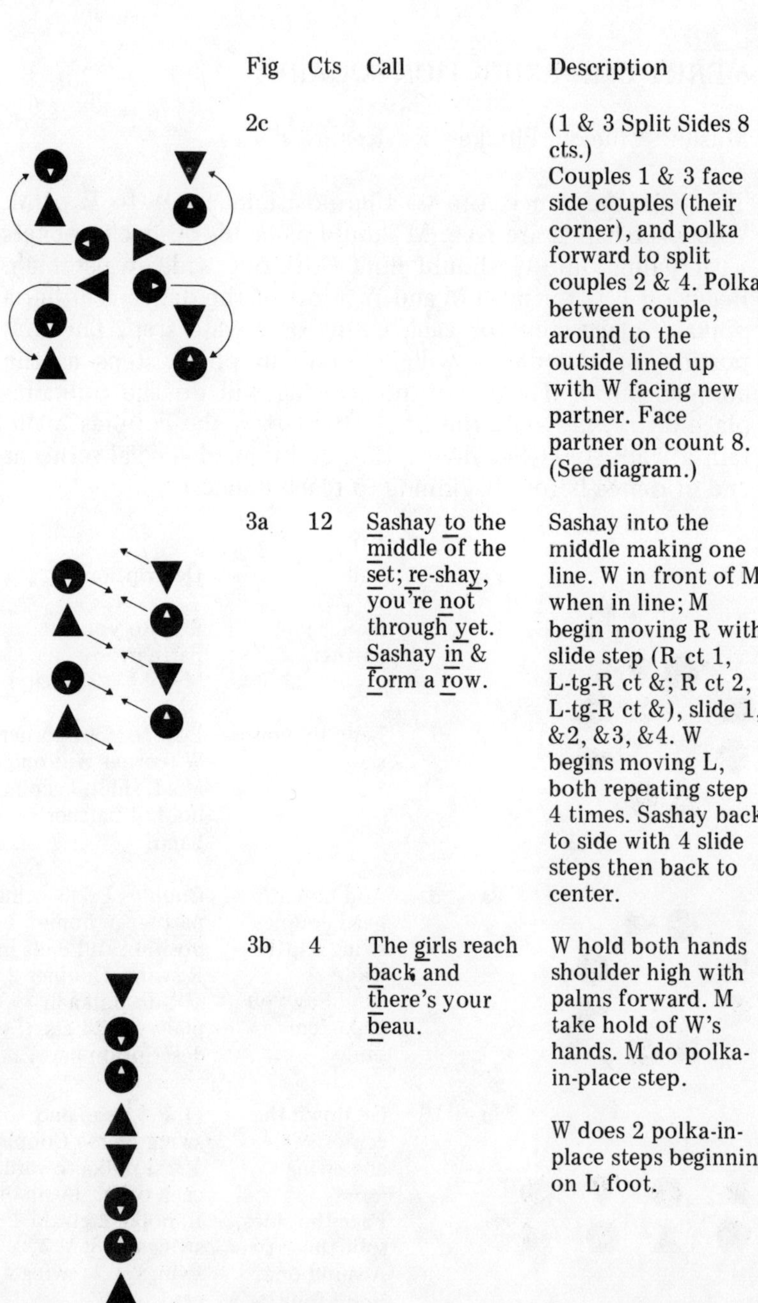

Fig	Cts	Call	Description
2c			(1 & 3 Split Sides 8 cts.) Couples 1 & 3 face side couples (their corner), and polka forward to split couples 2 & 4. Polka between couple, around to the outside lined up with W facing new partner. Face partner on count 8. (See diagram.)
3a	12	Sashay to the middle of the set; re-shay, you're not through yet. Sashay in & form a row.	Sashay into the middle making one line. W in front of M when in line; M begin moving R with slide step (R ct 1, L-tg-R ct &; R ct 2, L-tg-R ct &), slide 1, &2, &3, &4. W begins moving L, both repeating step 4 times. Sashay back to side with 4 slide steps then back to center.
3b	4	The girls reach back and there's your beau.	W hold both hands shoulder high with palms forward. M take hold of W's hands. M do polka-in-place step. W does 2 polka-in-place steps beginning on L foot.

Fig	Cts	Call	Description
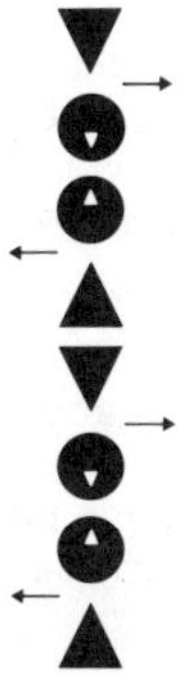 4	16	Heel, toe, out and then Heel, toe to the middle again Heel, toe, out you go Heel, toe and in you know.	(See description of heel-toe-polka.) Both M & W begin by hopping on R, L heel to side ct 1; hop R, point L toe across R on ct 2; slide sideward L with side-tg-side (LRL). Repeat, moving R; repeat step 4 times.
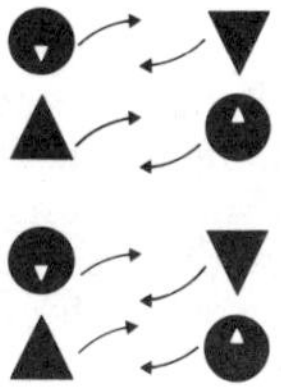 5	16	Sashay to places all Pass through across the hall; Right & left back on a heel & toe, Turn 'em around and don't be slow.	Sashay back to beginning places. M turn ¼ R, W turn ¼ L to face partner. Pass R thru across 4 cts doing polka; M step forward R, W on L, both turn ½ L to face opposite direction. Join RR contact on ct 9, repeat pass thru. M moves to L side of corner W on ct 12. Turn W L courtesy turn to face opposite couple, up and down stage in 4 cts. (See courtesy turn description.)
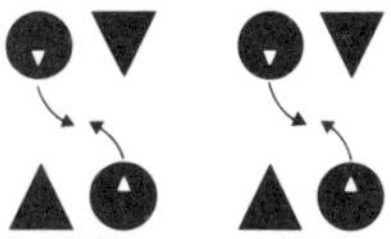 6	16	Chain the ladies down the line, Turn a girl you're doin' fine Chain 'em back on a heel and toe, Turn a little girl and now you know.	Girl move forward with polka step taking RR contact with opposite W passing R shoulders. Meet M across from you on ct 4, courtesy turn in 4 cts. Repeat. M do polka-in-place as ladies chain.

Fig	Cts	Call	Description
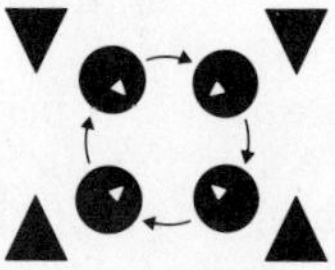 7a	8	Ladies chain across the set, Turn 'em boys, you're not thru yet.	W forms a R hand star to chain across the set with polka step, 4 cts. M & W do courtesy turn, 4 cts.
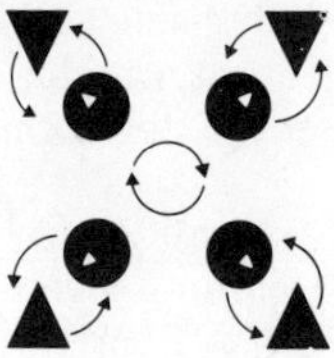 7b	8	Chain 'em back, now you go Turn 'em round, get ready Joe.	Repeat above and chain them back to beginning position. Courtesy turn W.
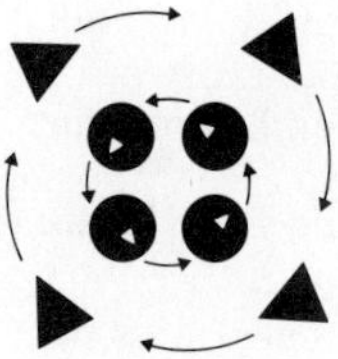 8	16	Ladies center form a ring Circle right like everything Men to the left and pass her by, Stoop low and lift her high.	W Polka to center, joining hands and move counterclockwise 8 cts. M Polka W moving clockwise, pick W up in a Rosette Lift. (See description of Rosette Lift.)
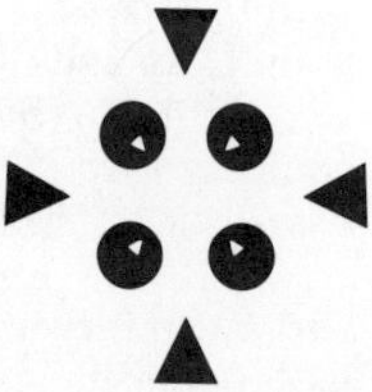 9	16	Girls fan out like a great big rose, Hold it there you take a pose; Hold tight and let her down, Her feet will touch the ground.	Rosette Lift M put W down in home position on counts 15 & 16.
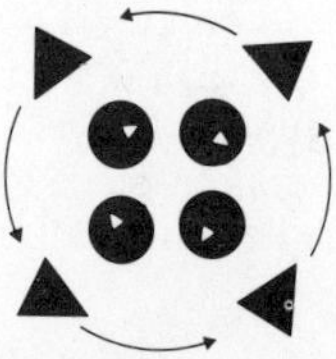 10a	8	Allemande left and the ladies star, The boys promenade you know.	Allemande L your corner, W go around corner and into center forming a R hand star moving clockwise. M walks counterclockwise 8

Fig	Cts	Call	Description
			cts moving ½ around square.
10b	8	Left allemande the gentlemen star, The girls run around that big old square.	Meet corner W doing allemande L and M go into center forming a right hand star moving clockwise; W walks counterclockwise for 8 cts.
11	16	Allemande left with the old left hand, Away you go with a right and left grand; Grand right and left around You meet your own and come on down.	Meet corner with allemande L; go right into a R & L grand. Couples face toward partner, join R hand, move forward, pass R shoulders. Without turning, join L hand with next person, passing L shoulders. Continue R L contact until you meet your partner. M proceed counterclockwise; W move clockwise. When you meet your partner M promenade W home. (See Promenade description.)
12a	16	It's join hands and circle right, Men step in, make a circle there; Pick your girl up in the air, Circle around and don't fall down.	M step to the center and join hands, 4 cts. W sits on M hands with W hands on M shoulders, W facing out & to R of partner. M pick up W in 4 cts.

Fig	Cts	Call	Description
12b	16	— — — — — — — — — — — — — — (Down on 15-16).	Merry-Go-Round Lift M walk clockwise for 16 cts with W in merry-go-round lift. (See merry-go-round lift description.) Lift is called for 16 cts but M must start putting W down after ct 12.
	8	Hey promenade don't slow down Promenade that's two by two.	Promenade. Separate to form king's cross.
13	8	The men reach in a left hand star, Pick up the girl right where you are.	4 cts for M to take L hand star, 4 cts to pick up girl. (This Figure can be done with 4 couples making king's cross.)
	16	It's a king's cross and don't get lost. — — — — — — — — — — — —	(See description of king's cross.) king's cross (16 cts in the air).
	4	Now put her down and swing at home.	Put ladies down in home position.
	12	Everybody swing your own Swing her high swing her low Swing a little girl in calico.	Swing partner for 12 cts in R buzz position (See description of buzz turn).

Fig	Cts	Call	Description
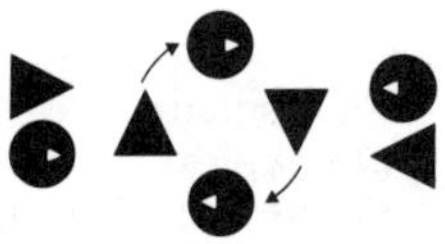 14a	8	Head couples star by the right, Pick up your corner arm around.	Couples 1 & 3 walk to the ctr, holding R hand high forming star; M in front of partner, walk clockwise 8 cts.
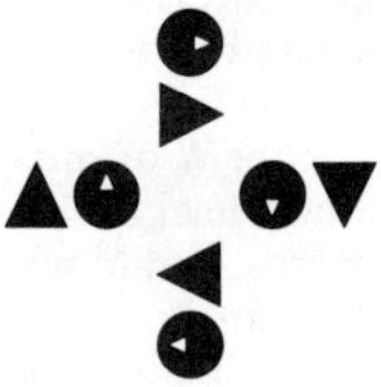 14b	8	Star prome-nade that town Take a little walk and then, —	M pick up corner W and W pick up corner M. L arm around their corner's waist, corner's arms around center couples. Star promenade 8 cts.
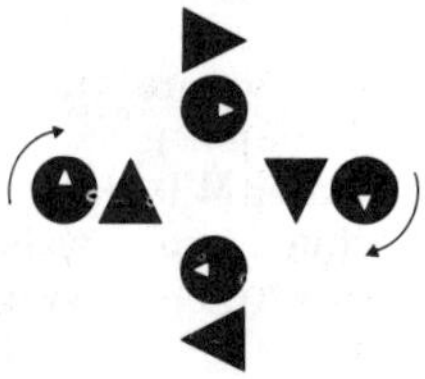 15a	8	Outside gent roll back one, Come on boys, have a little fun.	Outside M 4 & 2 do a L pivot turn making 2 complete turns in 4 cts, to be picked up by partner. M 4 should be directly opposite to begin pivot turn. Star continues moving clockwise 4 cts.
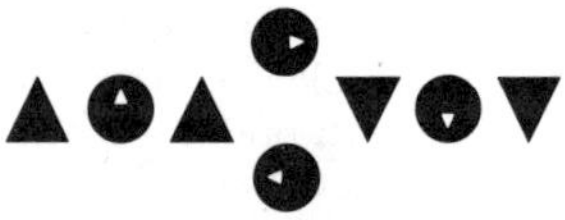 15b	8	The lonesome lady roll back, Keep on 'a goin' round the track.	W 1 should be directly in front of audience, W 3 opposite. Do a L pivot turn making 2 complete turns in 4 cts, to be picked up by M 4 & 2. Continue walking counterclockwise 4 cts into straight line.
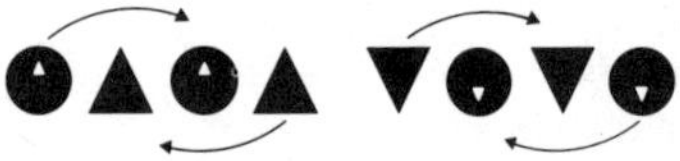 16a	8	Reverse that line Reverse that star You're goin' wrong	Center M wheel backwards, end W wheel forward holding lines of 4. Face opposite direction.

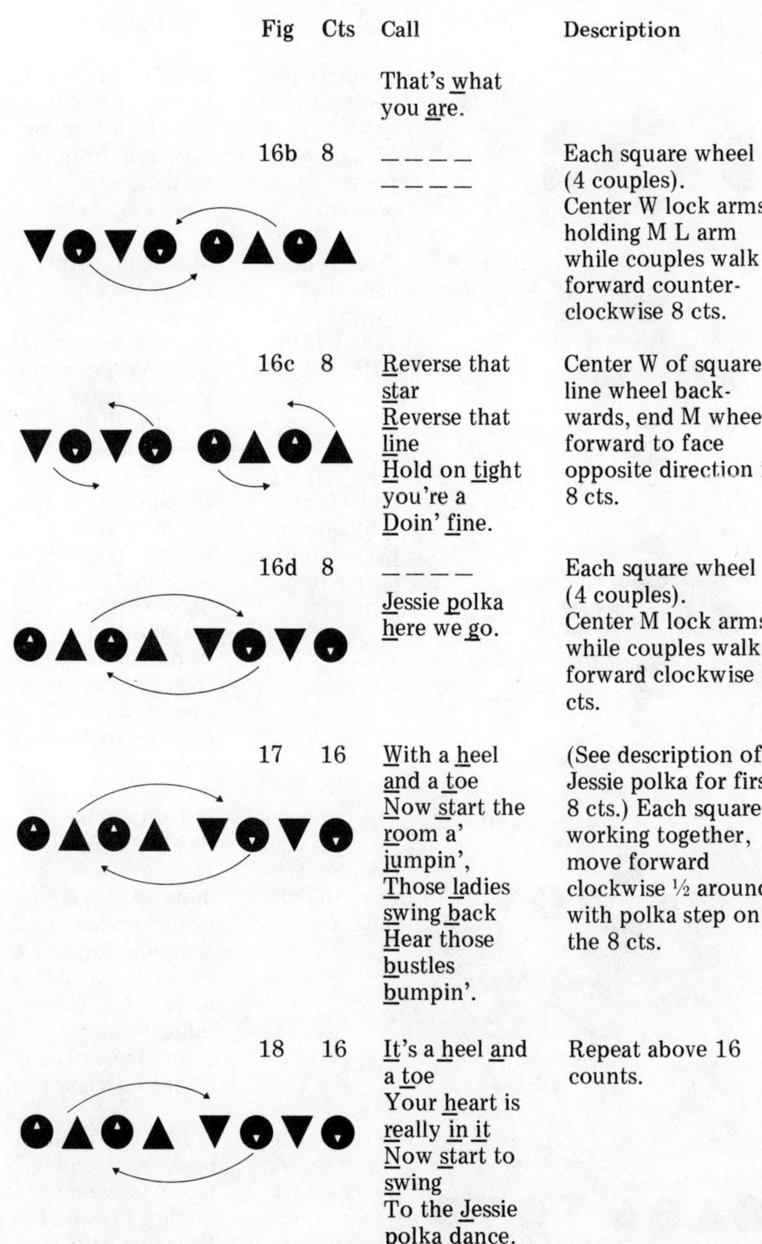

Fig	Cts	Call	Description
		That's what you are.	
16b	8	_ _ _ _ _ _ _ _	Each square wheel (4 couples). Center W lock arms holding M L arm while couples walk forward counter-clockwise 8 cts.
16c	8	Reverse that star Reverse that line Hold on tight you're a Doin' fine.	Center W of square line wheel backwards, end M wheel forward to face opposite direction in 8 cts.
16d	8	_ _ _ _ Jessie polka here we go.	Each square wheel (4 couples). Center M lock arms while couples walk forward clockwise 8 cts.
17	16	With a heel and a toe Now start the room a' jumpin', Those ladies swing back Hear those bustles bumpin'.	(See description of Jessie polka for first 8 cts.) Each square working together, move forward clockwise ½ around with polka step on the 8 cts.
18	16	It's a heel and a toe Your heart is really in it Now start to swing To the Jessie polka dance.	Repeat above 16 counts.

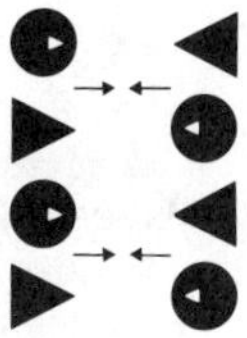

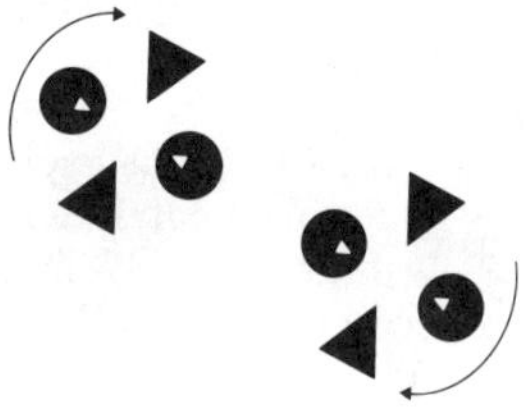

Fig	Cts	Call	Description
19	4	Well the men back out And form a line,	Still maintaining lines of four M back up to face across the line.
20	4	Circle forward, Circle back.	Circle clockwise with M 1 & W 3; M 4 & W 4 moving toward audience (downstage), W 3 leading out. Circle clockwise with M 3 & W 1; M 2 & W 2 moving opposite direction (upstage), W 1 leading out. Couples are on a diagonal.
20	8	Ladies bow, the gents know how, Pick 'em up and swing and whirl.	(See description of butterfly-flaps lift.) M should maintain smooth buzz turn for 16 cts.
	16	— — — — — — — — — — — — — — — —	Butterfly-flaps lift
	4	Now put her down and circle back.	Put W down in 4 cts.
	12	One big circle that's what you do, When you're home swing and whirl, Round and	W 3 & W 1 lead back to large circle into home position in 4 cts. Swing partner 8 cts doing 4 R buzz turns.

Fig	Cts	Call	Description
		round with the pretty little girl.	
21	16	(ENDING) — — — — — — — — — — (whirl out 11-12) Sit 13-14 Pose 15-16	M & W keep L R contact and whirl 10 cts. M arches W 1½ R turns on cts 11 & 12. All couples face downstage (audience). W kick R leg forward, falls back for M to catch her under arms. W sits on floor with R leg crossed over L leg on cts 13 & 14. W points R index finger to chin with L hand on R knee; M points R index finger at top of W's head, L hand on hip, R foot forward on cts 15 & 16. Swing 10, arch 11 & 12, W falls back on ct 13 & 14. Both point and hold pose ct 15-16.

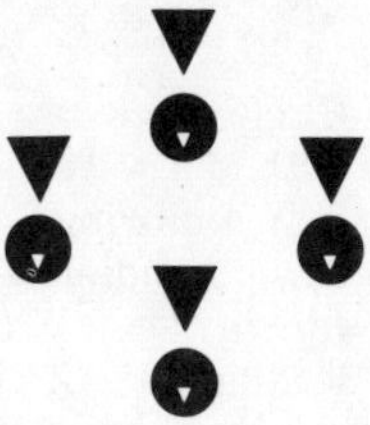

DESCRIPTION OF TERMINOLOGY USED IN EXHIBITION SQUARE DANCE

1. **Honor:** All M & W bow to their partners. (Honor your Corner): All M & W bow to their corners.

2. **Polka-in-place:** Start by touching the L heel in place (ct 1), then touch L toe in place (ct &); step on L ft (ct 2). A slight hop will be taken on the R ft as you do the L heel; hop on R ft as you do the L toe (or hop, hop on ct 1&). Touch R heel in place (ct 3), touch R toe in place (ct &). Step on R ft (ct 4), again hop on L ft as you touch R heel and hop as you touch R toe. (Ct 1&2, 3&4.)

3. **Polka:** The polka is often described as a two-step preceded by a hop. The step pattern is: hop, step, close, step, with the quick hop coming on the latter part of the upbeat.

4. **Swing:** Arm around swing; couple take square dance position (right-side position) and turn clockwise in place, using a shuffle walking step or buzz step. They usually complete two revolutions unless otherwise implied by music or call. Care should be taken to keep swing perfectly smooth (no bobbing up and down).

5. **Sashay:** This step is usually done as a slide step moving R or L. To sashay L, step on L moving L (ct 1), R tg L (ct &), moving L step L (ct 2)—each ct on L foot moving that direction. (Ct 1, &2, &3, &4.)

6. **Re-sashay:** Partner return to place, using same action as in sashay, beginning on opposite feet and moving in opposite direction.

7. **Heel-toe Polka:** If the L foot is the starting foot, the heel of the L foot is touched to the floor to the side, toe up (ct 1), then the toe of the same foot (L) is touched to the floor across R, heel up (ct 2). A slight hop may be

taken on the R foot as the L heel is placed to the side and again as the L toe is placed across R. The basic polka step starts on the L foot sliding sideward L (hop, side-tg-side – R-LRL).

8. **Chain:** ladies chain: Two couples face each other and the W join R hands as they pass each other to exchange places. W give L hand to opposite M and, assuming courtesy turn position, both wheel full L turn to face opposite couple. Chain right back: Repeat above action, W returning to partner.

9. **Four ladies chain:** Four Ws join R hand and star clockwise across the set to opposite M, assuming courtesy turn position and wheeling L into place. Repeat action to return to partners if call indicates.

10. **Courtesy turn:** Facing partner, M takes W's L hand in his L hand, places R hand behind her back, and holds her R hand on her R hip. Wheel left into place for next movement.

11. **Ocean wave:** This movement, is usually preceded by a call similar to "do-sa-do, all the way round to an ocean wave," the do-sa-do starts with the couples facing each other. They move forward around each other, passing right shoulders then back, passing left shoulders, doing a complete circle plus ¼ with girls ending in the middle of the line. The dancers are then in a line formation facing alternate directions with hands joined and the ladies in the center of the line. Each dancer then does a balance step.

12. **Balance:** The balance is performed when partners face each other, join R hands, take one step forward on L ft, bring R ft to L ft, then step on L ft in place. (LRL), then back on R ft, bring L ft to R ft, then step on R ft in place (RLR).

13. **Swing thru:** This is usually done from an ocean wave line (dancers facing alternate directions). On the call "Swing thru," they break in the middle and the end couples wheel clockwise half-way round. The new center two persons then join hands and wheel counterclockwise half-way around to make a new ocean wave line. If, at the beginning the men were on the ends of line, they are now in the center.

14. **Allemande left:** (on the corner) M grasps L wrist of corner W, the W on M's left, and they walk forward counterclockwise once around.

15. **Grand right and left:** Usually preceded by an allemande left. All couples face partners, grasp R wrist and move forward, passing R shoulders without turning, grasp L wrists with next person approaching, pass L shoulders, and continue action as long as call indicates. More commonly done until partners meet on opposite side to promenade, or continue all the way around to meet partner in home position for further action. M proceed counterclockwise, W clockwise, around circle.

16. **Promenade:** Both face same direction. W is to R of M. Left hands joined in front of M, R hands are joined in front of W with M's R arm above W's L arm. W should keep L arm straight while M keeps R arm straight. Arms are held chest high.

17. **Star:** Persons designated join either R or L hands (as indicated by call) in center of set and move forward to make star revolve.

18. **Pick up:** To break circle or line to include designated person or persons. Caution: care should be taken to pick up new additions in their proper place. Lead M or person always breaks with person to his L to provide opening.

19. **Jessie polka:** (*Figure 31*) Heel of L ft touches floor in front (ct 1), hop on both feet together (ct 2), point R

Figure 31

toe back (ct 3), hop on both feet together (ct 4), kick R ft forward (ct 5), leap onto R ft and extend L ft back (ct 6), touch L heel to floor in front (ct 7), and cross L ft over R and touch L toe at side of R ft (ct 8). Remember to maintain a hop throughout the step.

20. **Buzz turn:** Left buzz turn is done stepping on L foot and paddle-turning around to the left by pushing with R foot. To do a R buzz turn, step on the R ft and paddle-turn to the right by pushing with the L foot.

21. **Pass right through:** Cross over and exchange places with opposite person, passing R shoulders. Upon reaching opposite position each turns R singly.

22. **Right & left through:** Couples pass through each other to exchange places. As they approach, grasp R hand of opposite person and pass R shoulders. When opposite couples are back to back, they grasp L hand of partner and assume courtesy turn position and make L turn in place.

Figure 32

DESCRIPTION OF LIFTS USED IN "EXHIBITION SQUARE '73"

Rosette:

(*Figure 32.*)

Four couples. W join hands in the center. M stand to the left of partner. M bend down enough for W to sit on M's arms. M put right arm around back of partner's legs, holding onto her right leg just above the knee. M on right side of W then holds other M's elbow, so M's right arm holds partner's right leg; M's left hand holds other M's right elbow (which has hold of his own partner's right leg). W face toward center and lock legs across. W 1 and 3 lock legs first, by putting right leg in center and left leg on outside. Cross ankles over opposite W's leg and extend legs so opposite W almost sits on other's feet. W 2 and 4 then lock legs under the locked legs of 1 and 3 in the same manner. M revolve left (clockwise), with an even walk step. With hands still joined, W lean back and out as far as possible so head and shoulders are outside circle. Duplicate above pattern for other half of set. *Caution: Be most careful that girls do not fan out until their legs are securely locked!*

Figure 33

Merry-go-round:
(*Figure 33.*)
Four couples. All four M face center and join hands, right to left. M should hold hands in this manner: (decide whose hand is on top or bottom) Top hand grasps little finger of bottom hand between thumb and index finger. Bottom hand grasps wrist. Top hand palm down and bottom hand palm up. W sit on M's hands and place hands on M's shoulders. W are to right of partner and facing out. M walk clockwise in circle facing forward. For 16 counts W ride in place. W 1 begins waving right hand when she faces audience, then each W waves until lift ride is over. M begin putting W down on count 13; all down by count 16. Duplicate above pattern for other half of set.

King's cross:
(*Figures 34a, 34b.*)
Two couples facing opposite direction. M have left shoulders together, with partners on their right. M cross left arms behind each other's back; place right arm around W's waist, grasping her right hip firmly. W's left arm is over partner's right arm and grasps opposite M's left wrist with her left hand

Figure 34a

Figure 34b

behind partner's back. He grasps her left wrist with his left hand. (Pivot point is between the two M.) M walk forward counterclockwise in a "weathervane" motion and as the momentum picks up, her feet fly. W arches back, her right hand holding skirt out. As M rotate, they lean away from each other. W must keep back arched. Duplicate above pattern for balance of set.

Figure 35

Butterfly flaps:
(*Figure 35.*)
Two couples form four sides of a small square with M facing each other and W facing each other. W is to right of partner. Partners are: M 1 and W 3; M 4 and W 4; M 3 and W 1; M 2 and W 2. M places right hand around partner's waist, then with left hand, takes hold of second M's right elbow. W places one hand on each M's shoulder closest to her, and NOT around the neck to the other shoulder. (This helps take the weight.) W arch back as M do quick, smooth, buzz steps to the left (clockwise). The W's feet will fly up, and the turn should be kept even. As soon as the W's feet fly up, M begin the flaps by moving their arms in an even up and down motion. The flaps are done with the M's arms and not by any other body movement. W should keep their heads straight (not back), and bend head to the left so as not to hit the W's head across from her. Duplicate above pattern for balance of set.

12. Test and Evaluate Your Knowledge

WRITTEN TEST

(This phase of the tests counts 100 points: 94–100 = Excellent, 88–93 = Good, 78–87 = Average, 72–77 = Fair, Below 72 = Poor.)

A. Circle T if the statement is true, F if the statement is false. (1 point each)

T F 1. Square dance is considered an American folk dance.
T F 2. In the square, the couple nearest the music is couple number three.
T F 3. Couples number two and four are called head couples.
T F 4. In the square formation, couples are numbered in a clockwise direction.
T F 5. In the square formation, the lady on the left is the man's corner lady.
T F 6. Square dance is very dynamic in the sense that it is constantly undergoing change.
T F 7. In a grand right and left the ladies move clockwise.
T F 8. To perform the elbow swing, the man's right arm and the lady's left arm are hooked together at the elbows.
T F 9. In the courtesy-turn position, the two dancers are side by side and facing the same direction.
T F 10. A right-hand star rotates in a counterclockwise direction unless otherwise directed by the caller.
T F 11. Posture is not an important factor in square dancing.
T F 12. It is a good idea to memorize square dance routines so that you need not listen carefully to the caller.
T F 13. The grand right and left begins with partners joining right hands.
T F 14. The grand right and left must be preceded by an allemande left.
T F 15. Weave the ring starts by passing left shoulders with your partner.
T F 16. In the half-promenade the active couples move around the outside of the square.

T F 17. In the promenade half way around, the active couples move around the inside of the square.

T F 18. In a two ladies' chain, the active ladies join left hands as they pass by each other.

T F 19. After a four ladies' chain, the ladies are with their opposite men.

T F 20. In the pass thru, the active couples pass left shoulders with the couples facing them.

T F 21. In the cross trail, the man passes behind his partner after doing a pass thru.

T F 22. In the half sashay, the lady moves in front of her partner.

T F 23. To perform a frontier whirl, the couple joins hands, man's left and lady's right.

T F 24. In the grand square, each dancer walks around an individual square with four steps on each side of the square.

T F 25. The turn-back movement causes a dancer to reverse directions.

T F 26. While in a left-hand star, the dancers rotate counterclockwise unless otherwise directed.

T F 27. In a star promenade, the ladies usually form the hub, and men form the rim.

T F 28. In the allemande-thar formation the men face opposite directions from the ladies.

T F 29. It is not possible to shoot the star from an allemande-thar formation.

T F 30. Throw in the clutch is a method of moving out of the star-promenade position.

T F 31. In the dip and dive, the head couples move in a counterclockwise direction while the side couples move clockwise.

T F 32. The ends-turn-in movement is performed from a line-of-four formation with dancers facing outward.

T F 33. At the completion of the substitute movement, the couples which dived under become the active couples.

T F 34. In the ocean wave, each dancer balances forward in the direction he is facing, then balances backward.

T F 35. In a bend the line, those on the end of the line move backward while those in the middle move forward.
T F 36. In the wheel and deal, the couple on the left moves in front of the couple on the right.
T F 37. In an all-eight chain, the man joins right hands with the first lady he meets and courtesy turns the second lady.
T F 38. In the eight-chain thru, each person completes the movement in the same position he started from.
T F 39. The double elbow combines the catch-all eight with the grand right and left.
T F 40. The Dixie chain starts from a single-file formation with men standing in front of their partners.
T F 41. Do-si-do and do-sa-do are the same movements.
T F 42. The Alamo style and the ocean wave both involve a balance forward and a balance back.
T F 43. The do-paso starts with partners joining right hands and walking around each other.
T F 44. In the circulate, each dancer progresses one-fourth of the way around the square.
T F 45. In the wagon wheel the men form a right-hand star.
T F 46. When the sides divide, each member of a side couple meets his opposite at a position vacated by the head couples.
T F 47. Active couples are those actively engaged in performing a movement at the particular moment.
T F 48. Fill-in calls are those which command the dancers to perform a movement.
T F 49. Foot couples and side couples are the same.
T F 50. Indian style is the same as single file.
T F 51. Patter calls are generally done to music which has a weak melody.
T F 52. "Those who can" refers to any dancer who is in position to perform the movement called.
T F 53. Because of the rustic background through which square dance developed, etiquette is unimportant to the activity.
T F 54. In promenade position, the left hands are on top.
T F 55. When the do-paso call is given, you turn your part-

ner with the left hand, corner with the right, and partner with the left.

T F 56. When you box the gnat, you face your partner and change places while holding right hands.

T F 57. When you swat the flea, you change places while holding left hands.

T F 58. When the call "grand square" is given, the side couples go into the center and the head couples back away from each other.

T F 59. Weave the ring means to do a grand right and left without touching hands.

T F 60. When the four ladies chain, the men remain at their home position.

T F 61. When the couple three lead to the left, they meet couple number one.

T F 62. When the girls star three-quarters 'round from home position, they end up with their opposite gent.

T F 63. California twirl and frontier whirl can be called for the same movement.

T F 64. You always meet your partner with your right hand in a grand right and left.

T F 65. The person you start a do-paso with becomes your partner at the completion of the movement.

T F 66. Fill-in calls command a dancer to perform a particular movement.

T F 67. An inappropriate command is a call given when the dancers are not in position to perform the movement.

T F 68. A figure done in arky style is performed by two dancers of the same sex.

B. Write *yes* if the call is possible; write *no* if the call is not possible. (2 points each)

1. ________ The call has been given for the head couples to square thru three quarters round. Can the next call be eight-chain thru?

2. ________ One and three do a half sashay, then up to the center and back that way. Give a right to the

opposite, box the gnat; can the next call be right and left thru?

3. ______ Head two couples go forward and back, cross trail thru, you turn back, half square thru after that. Can you call a left allemande?
4. ______ Two and four go up and back, half square thru across the track. Can you call swing your corner, go 'round and 'round?
5. ______ One and three do a half square thru, then half square thru with the outside two. Can the next call be bend the line?
6. ______ One and three star thru. Can the next call be frontier whirl?
7. ______ Two and four star thru, frontier whirl. Can the next call be eight chain thru?
8. ______ Heads wheel around to a right and left thru, come right back with a dixie chain, lady goes left, gent goes right. Can the next call be left allemande?
9. ______ One and three lead to the right, circle to a line. Can the next call be bend the line?
10. ______ Face your partner, box the gnat then box it back. Can the next call be grand right and left?
11. ______ One and three wheel around and square thru three-quarters 'round. Can the next call be cross trail, find your corner, left allemande?

C. Fill in the spaces with the correct words. (1 point each)

1. The head couples are numbers ______ and ______.
2. The side couples are numbers ______ and ______.
3. The foot pattern used in beginning square dance is a ______ step.
4. When you do-sa-do your partner, you pass ______.
5. When you see-saw your corner, you pass ______ shoulders first.
6. At the beginning of a dixie chain, the ladies are standing ______ their partners.
7. On the command "circulate," each dancer advances ______ of the way around the square.
8. To do a California whirl, the two dancers join hands,

man's __________ and lady's __________.

9. In a weave the ring, the men ordinarily move in a __________ direction around the square.
10. In a substitute, the __________ couples arch while the remaining couples dive under.

PERFORMANCE TEST

(100 points: 94—100 = Excellent, 86—93 = Good, 78-85 = Fair, Below 78 = Poor.)

Under this section perform each movement in the order listed. Then turn to chapter 4 to check your accuracy. Place a check opposite each movement you performed correctly.

A. With a partner perform the following. (4 points each)

_____ 1. Do-sa-do
_____ 2. All around left-hand lady
_____ 3. See-saw
_____ 4. Half-promenade
_____ 5. Balance
_____ 6. Courtesy turn
_____ 7. Sashay
_____ 8. Box the gnat
_____ 9. Swat the flea
_____ 10. Frontier whirl
_____ 11. Star thru
_____ 12. California twirl

B. With a partner and another couple do the following. (4 points each)

_____ 1. Two ladies chain
_____ 2. Pass thru
_____ 3. Cross trail
_____ 4. Right and left thru
_____ 5. Right-hand star
_____ 6. Ends turn in
_____ 7. Substitute
_____ 8. Ocean wave
_____ 9. Swing thru
_____ 10. Bend the line
_____ 11. Dixie chain
_____ 12. Do-si-do
_____ 13. Ends turn out

ANSWERS TO WRITTEN TESTS

Section A

1. T	11. F	21. T	31. T	41. F	51. T	61. F
2. F	12. F	22. T	32. T	42. T	52. T	62. F
3. F	13. T	23. F	33. T	43. F	53. F	63. T
4. F	14. F	24. T	34. T	44. T	54. F	64. T
5. T	15. F	25. T	35. F	45. F	55. T	65. T
6. T	16. F	26. T	36. F	46. T	56. T	66. F
7. T	17. F	27. F	37. T	47. T	57. T	67. T
8. F	18. F	28. T	38. T	48. F	58. F	68. T
9. T	19. T	29. F	39. T	49. T	59. T	
10. F	20. F	30. F	40. F	50. T	60. T	

Section B

1. no, 2. yes, 3. yes, 4. no, 5. yes, 6. yes, 7. yes, 8. yes, 9. yes, 10. yes, 11. yes.

Section C

1. one-three, 2. two-four, 3. walking, 4. right, 5. left, 6. in front of, 7. one-fourth, 8. right-left, 9. counterclockwise, 10. inside.

Glossary

This glossary does not include all of the terms that need to be defined because many of the terms are defined in the content of the chapters. For terms not included in the glossary, refer to the index.

Active Couple: The couple performing a particular movement at a given time. If the caller directs the head couples to perform a right and left through, the head couples would become active; the side couples would be inactive.

Appropriate Command: Any command to perform a movement the dancers are in position to perform.

Along the Line: Dancers often find themselves in line formation, such as two lines of four facing each other. When this is the case, the caller may command them to perform the movement along the line, meaning the dancers are to move in the direction of the line, rather than across the set to the opposite line.

Arky Style: A figure done by two dancers of the same sex working together as a couple.

Balance: Partners face each other and join either one or both hands, then take one step forward and close with the other foot, then step back and close.

Basic: A generally accepted, time-tested movement.

Break: The command to let go of hands in preparation for the next movement.

Buzz Step: The dancers assume a swing position with the two right feet placed close to each other to form a point of pivot and with the upper body leaning away. The left feet are used to push the dancer around the pivot in a manner similar to pushing a child's scooter.

Closer (ending): A sequence of square dance movements which follow the figure (or main portion) of the dance.

Command Calls: Calls that direct the dancers to perform specific movements, as opposed to nonsense and fill-in calls.

Corner: The person standing next to a dancer on the side opposite his partner in a square formation. A man's partner is on his right, and his corner is on his left. The reverse is true in the case of the ladies.

Figure: A sequence of square dance movements which ends with the men at their home positions. (The women are also usually at their beginning positions at the end of a figure.) The figure (or figures) composes the main portion of the dance.

Fill-In Calls: Calls given between command calls. They do not direct the dancers to perform movements, but give continuity to the calls.

Foot Couples: Couples number two and four, more commonly referred to as side couples.

Hash: A collection of parts of different figures arranged in an appropriate sequence.

Heads: Often used to refer to head couples; couples number one and three.

Hoedown Music: See patter music.

Home Position (Home Station): The position from which the couples started the dance. Actually, the ladies do not have home positions since they change partners throughout the dance.

Honors: The men bow and the ladies curtsy.

Hub: In a star-promenade or allemande-thar position, the star formed by the inside dancers.

Inappropriate Command: A command to perform a movement that the dancers are not in position to execute.

Indian Style: The same as single file. Dancers move around in the ring in a single-file formation.

Opener: A preliminary sequence of square dance movements which precede the figure (or main portion) of the dance.

Opposite: The person facing you in the dance formation.

Patter Music: Music with a strong beat and very little melody.

Patter (Talking) Calls: Calls done to music that has little melody and serves mainly as rhythmic background. The caller does not follow the melody.

Pull Her By: Two dancers facing each other join right or left hands and pull each other by, then move on as directed by the next call.

Rim: The outside persons in either a star promenade or an allemande thar.

Sequence: The numerical order of the men in the square. The men are numbered in a counterclockwise direction, 1, 2, 3, 4.

Set: Four couples in a square-dance formation.

Sides (Side Couples): Couples two and four.

Singing (Melody) Calls: Calls done to music with a melody which the caller must follow. These calls are written specifically for the melody.

Square: A set of four dance couples in a square formation.

Swap: Exchange partners with the one you are directed to swap with.

Tip: Two or three successive dances followed by rest periods.

Those Who Can: Those so situated at the time of the call that they can execute the movement. This assumes that some of the dancers are not in position to perform the movement.

Twirl: A man and a lady facing each other join right (or left) hands and the man turns the lady under his raised right (or left) arm.

Walking Step (Swing): The dancers assume a swing position with the feet close together and leaning away with the upper body. The dancers walk smoothly around a tight circle in time to the music.

Wrong Way 'Round: A circling movement in the opposite direction from which the movement is normally performed. For instance, in the grand right and left, the men normally move counterclockwise. In the wrong way 'round right and left grand, the men move in a clockwise direction.

You Turn Back: An individual facing movement to reverse direction.

Bibliography

BOOKS, PAMPHLETS, AND PERIODICALS

American Squares. 1159 Broad Street, Newark, New Jersey.

Caller's Guide. Square Dance Callers' Association of Southern California, P. O. Box 1024, South Gate, California.

Hall, J. Tillman. *Dance! A Complete Guide to Social, Folk and Square Dancing*. Belmont, California: Wadsworth Publishing Company, 1963.

Harris, Jane; Pittman, Anne; and Waller, Marlys S., *Dance A While*. Minneapolis: Burgess Publishing Company, 1964.

Sets in Order. National square-dance magazine, 462 N. Robertson Blvd., Los Angeles, California, 90048. (Sets in Order also offers the following pamphlets: *Story of Square Dancing*; *Record Party Handbook*; *Square Dance Party Fun*; *Club Organization Handbook*; *Indoctrination Handbook*; *Basic Movements of Square Dancing*.)

Shaw, Lloyd, *Cowboy Dances*. Caldwell, Idaho: Caxton Printers Ltd., 1945.

Training Manual. Square Dance Callers' Association of Southern California, P. O. Box 1024, South Gate, California.

RECORD COMPANIES

Blue Star Records, P. O. Box 7308, Houston, Tex.

Educational Record Sales, 157 Chambers Street, New York, N.Y. 10007.

Folkcraft Record Company, 1159 Broad Street, Newark, N. J. 10011.

Grenn, Inc., P. O. Box 216, Bath, Ohio 44210.

Hi Hat, Box 69833, Los Angeles, Calif. 90069.

Honor Your Partner Records, Educational Activities, Inc., P. O. Box 392, Freeport, N. Y. 11520.

Imperial Records, 137 N. Western Ave., Los Angeles, Calif.

J-Bar-L Records, Sets in Order, 462 N. Robertson Blvd., Los Angeles, Calif. 90048.

Jubilee Records, 8811 N. 38 Dr., Phoenix, Ariz. 85021.

Kalox Records, 316 Starr St., Dallas, Tex.

MacGregor Company, 729 Western Ave., Hollywood, Calif. 90005.

Old Timer Records, P. O. Box 64343, Los Angeles, Calif. 90064.

Wagon Wheel Records, 9500 53rd Ave., Arvada, Colo. 80002.

Windsor Record Company, Temple City, Calif.